WINNING AFTER THE GAME

WINNING
AFTER
THE GAME

HOW TO WIN
IN YOUR LIFE
NO MATTER WHO
YOU ARE OR
WHAT YOU'VE
BEEN THROUGH

SETEMA GALI

NEW YORK

NASHVILLE • MELBOURNE • VANCOUVER

WINNING AFTER THE GAME
HOW TO WIN IN YOUR LIFE NO MATTER WHO YOU ARE OR WHAT YOU'VE BEEN THROUGH

Published in New York, New York, by Morgan James Publishing. Morgan James is a trademark of Morgan James, LLC. www.MorganJamesPublishing.com

The Morgan James Speakers Group can bring authors to your live event. For more information or to book an event visit The Morgan James Speakers Group at www.TheMorganJamesSpeakersGroup.com.

ISBN 978-1-68350-488-7 paperback
ISBN 978-1-68350-489-4 eBook
Library of Congress Control Number: 2017903217

Cover Design by:
Rachel Lopez
www.r2cdesign.com

Interior Design by:
Bonnie Bushman
The Whole Caboodle Graphic Design

In an effort to support local communities, raise awareness and funds, Morgan James Publishing donates a percentage of all book sales for the life of each book to Habitat for Humanity Peninsula and Greater Williamsburg.

Get involved today! Visit
www.MorganJamesBuilds.com

"Victorious warriors win first and then go to war, while defeated warriors go to war first and then seek to win."
—Sun Tzu

Table of Contents

Foreword by Scott L. Byrd   ix

Preface by Ryan Stewman   xii

Introduction   xiv

Acknowledgements   xix

Chapter 1   Crossing the Ocean   1

Chapter 2   Weak Body, Strong Dreams: The Power of   9
             Clarity to Create Change

Chapter 3   Wounded but Healing: Lessons in Selfless   21
             Love and Loving Self

Chapter 4   Walking by Faith, Not by Sight: The Only   31
             Way to See Is to Go through It

Chapter 5   The Seeds of Greatness Arise through Adversity: 39
             Embrace It and Love It

Chapter 6   The Truth about Gifts: "Seek Ye the Best Gifts"   47

Chapter 7   Iron Sharpens Iron: The Catalyst of Brotherhood   55

Chapter 8   Starting Over, but Not Really: Using the Past to   65
             Propel the Future

Chapter 9   God Sends an Angel: When a Man Loves a Woman   75

Chapter 10 Wilderness and Despair: What You Don't Know   87
            or Don't Admit Will Destroy You

Chapter 11 What's Old Is New Again: Rediscovering the Grind   99

Chapter 12 Rebuilding on Sweat Equity: Commitment   117
            Alters Everything

Chapter 13 When It's Time to Walk Away, Do It: 125
            The Faith to Leap

Chapter 14 Lessons in Leading: To Lead, First Be Led   135

Chapter 15 The Golden Thread: Learning to Love the Voice   143

Chapter 16 What's Next For You In The Game Of Life?   153

Foreword

by Scott L. Byrd

I'll never forget where I was when Setema called me the first time. It was a chilly January morning on the island where I live in the low country of South Carolina. I was standing on the front porch of my home, pondering a morning full of intense coaching conversations. Completely lost in thought, a Utah number popped up on my phone. Now, like most of people, I'll typically send an unknown number like this to voicemail. For some reason, I accepted the call. It was at that very moment a friendship was born that will last forever.

The purpose for the call was simple, he was looking for his next personal coach. Less than one hour later of being together on the phone, he requested a coaching relationship with me. To this day, Setema is the only person I have ever accepted as a client on the first call. There was simply no question that this was a man on a mission and I was deeply moved to be a part of it.

It was clear from the first day of our work together that this man was different from any other client I had had to date. He had already been coached by some of the world's top athletic coaches. Quickly, I learned of his time with Coach Bill Belichick while he was a player with the New England Patriots. We spoke of his days of domination at Brigham Young University and how he had overcome adversity to be one of the top collegiate players in the world. We explored his deep desire to serve the world through his demonstration of leadership and power. And finally, despite years of devastating hardship through the economic crisis of 2008-2009, Setema came to me passionately committed to fulfilling the calling from his God to enter into the world of elite, personal performance coaching.

And, our work began. While it would be inappropriate to share the intimate details of our work together, it would be fair to say it was brutally intense at times. Even with the consistent intensity, Setema brought himself to each session with razor sharp focus, clear intention and a desire that demonstrated why he had been so successful in almost everything he had accomplished in his life. He was clear on his mission of mastery.

And, he was humble. Always open and hungry to what was possible in our time together. When we co-created powerful agreements he brought himself fully to our commitment to each other. He made me a better man through our work together.

Setema is a leader. Period. Although many get enamored with his pure physical size, his uncanny resemblance to the Rock, and his Super Bowl ring, I don't see all of this. Through our work together I discovered a powerful, humble, loving human being who intensely desires to serve. I discovered a man completely devoted to his family and his faith. And, I discovered a man committed to performing at the highest levels of human achievement no matter what it takes.

And finally, Setema Gali is a world class coach. Can this really be a surprise? Any of you reading this who have experienced the power of working with him can easily attest. He has worked with my wife, Angie. I'll never forget the day my wife came home from a week long training with Setema. When she returned from that trip, the tears in her eyes told me everything I needed to know. This man makes a powerful impact on peoples' lives. This man makes a difference. I love this man.

Now to the book you are about to read. I challenge you to devour it. Learn about this man. Draw inspiration and power for your own life through his words. Setema is a gifted writer and orator. For those of you inclined towards personal development, take these words in and experience what is possible in your own life. As a performance coach myself, I so appreciate being able to discover what makes a powerful man tick. I can't get enough of the experiences each of us has that shape and form our life's creation.

Especially when that person moves through the world as powerfully as Setema.

This book is a beautiful demonstration of power, purpose, prosperity, and faith.

It will move you.

Scott L. Byrd
Co-Founder
Ontocore

Preface

by Ryan Stewman

When you meet Setema in person, you get that "good guy" energy from him immediately. I remember when I saw him with his family the first night we met; I watched as his kids tackled him with a full sprint and all I could think was, *I hope my kids love me half as much as those kids love Setema.*

Setema is one of the guys you want on your side. You know that no matter what he does, he's going to work hard enough to eventually win at it. And win BIG. After all, you don't become a Super Bowl champion without firsthand knowledge of what hard work really is.

Setema has been called to write this book his whole life, and now here it is. It's tough to tell the real story. Writing a book like this takes heart. Putting these words together can bring a man to tears. It brought me to tears and I don't cry easily, rarely if ever. Setema poured his heart and soul into the words you are about to read—and with good reason.

I've known Setema for years now, and I can tell you with 100 percent conviction that he lives his life exactly how he tells it to you. He's the real deal, which is why this book is so powerful. He shares a story that will instill hope in your heart, and show you that if you keep dreaming and working hard, those goals will manifest in your life. Setema is just another perfect example of how, when you put your mind to it, you can accomplish anything you want.

Ryan Stewman, "The Hardcore Closer"
Founder
Break Free Academy

Introduction

Sweat, heat, sun…

Pushing myself to exhaustion…

Going all out… rep after rep… all day long…

Sweat, heat, sun…

Driven by deep purpose and inner fire…

Sweat, heat, sun…

Going all out… rep after rep… all day long…

Get knocked down… get back up.

Sounds like an athlete putting in hours of practice, preparing to play the game at the highest level. As a professional football player for the New England Patriots, I know that path well—the path of sacrifice and unrelenting determination.

But this moment of heat, sweat, and grind did not occur on the football field. It happened on the streets of southern Georgia. No helmet, jersey, or shoulder pads. Instead, I wore a bright orange polo shirt and a baseball cap, and I held a clipboard as I went door-to-door selling security and home automation systems for Vivint.

Door after door...

Knock after knock...

Sweat, heat, sun...

Rep after rep... all day long...

Yes, brothers and sisters, going from winning the Super Bowl and running a seven-figure mortgage and real estate business to asking people if they want to buy a smart home alarm system—that took some getting used to. I never ate lunch on those knocking days because I was already filled up on extra servings of humble pie.

Yet, it was right there, on those furnace-like streets, far, far away from the stadium lights, fans, and trophies... it was there that IT happened.

It began just like any other day as I lifted my hand for the thousandth time to knock on another nameless, faceless door when I saw it—the empty space on my finger; the empty void where my Super Bowl ring should have been.

You see, a year earlier, after my mortgage business had failed, after the bank accounts were emptied, the cars were sold, and the homes foreclosed on, my wife came to me in tears and said, "Setema, I love you, but there's no food in the house. What are you going to do?"

Five days later, I was on a plane to New York to exchange my Super Bowl ring (the only thing I had left that had any monetary value) for an envelope full of cash. I sobbed like a baby the whole flight.

I stepped off the plane, took the cash, gave the collector my ring, and then and there, I knew it was most likely gone forever. My ring was gone. The one thing every kid dreams of, that every football player would die for, that every legend is judged by—I'd just sold it so I could buy some groceries and pay my rent. It's tough to describe how I felt at that moment. Angry and bitter don't quite do it justice.

It was my blood, sweat, and tears that had earned that ring, and now it was sitting on some rich guy's mantle, locked up in a glass case like a trinket—just one more ring among a collection of hundreds.

And why? Because he had money and I didn't. Plain and simple. End of story.

So, I went home from New York determined that I was never going to feel that way again. Never again would a lack of money define my value as a human being.

I picked myself up. I swallowed my pride and went to work, doing the only thing I was qualified to do that could bring me a lot of money: selling security systems door-to-door.

And yes, my friends, it was right then and there... away from my home, away from my family and stripped of any remaining shreds of fame, success, and glory that I found IT. I found something that lifted me out of the hell of depression and self-loathing, that healed me from the shame of my downfall, that liberated me from the chains of my own self-definition.

I found my **holy cause**.

I saw that empty finger and instead of seeing shame, I saw the love of my wife, Laina. I saw the precious faces of my two young sons at the time. I saw the sacrifice of my father and mother who worked and scraped for years to immigrate from Samoa to the United States so their children could have better lives.

Instead of despair and embarrassment, I saw unrestrained love and energy flowing to me from a God who still knew me, who still loved me, and was waiting patiently for me to remember who I was.

In that moment a modern-day miracle occurred, the greatest miracle any of us can ever experience—my heart changed. *I believed again.* I saw my future as one full of prosperity, abundance, power, and greatness, and I believed that it could happen. I saw possibility.

I wanted to be wealthy because I was done being poor. I wanted to be successful because I wanted to take care of my wife. I wanted to be a leader to show my sons through example that anything is possible, that they could create whatever they wanted in their lives no matter how much they'd been through.

Most of all, I wanted to rise up and do what I felt God had put me on this earth to do—to live a life of love, power, and certainty, and to lead and liberate others to do the same.

Over the last five years I have been on an unrelenting journey through grief and pain, hope and belief, confidence and hustle—and finally to a permanent state of power and certainty.

This book recounts my story from little league to the NFL... from a Super Bowl championship to bankruptcy... from being a million-dollar producer in the mortgage business to a door-to-door salesman.

Most of all, the book documents the principles, insights, and distinctions I gained along the way—principles that have become the foundation of a modern-day movement known as "The Prosperity Revolution."

I invite you to come along with me on this journey of destruction, redemption, and power—not to be entertained by my story, but to open yourself to the insights, truths, and impressions you'll experience along the way. These impressions will guide you to getting clear on what it is you truly want to create in your life.

And if you listen deeply to the voice that's guiding you, I promise you can experience your own modern-day miracle. You, too, can see the future ahead of you clearly, a future of pure abundance and endless expansion, and know without a doubt that you can create it. I am a creator and you are, too.

Yes, brothers and sisters, it is far, far away from the lights, the crowds, and the performances of our lives that we truly find ourselves—that we learn how to truly live and "Win After The Game."

The Revolution has begun.

Join me.

Setema Gali
The Reverend of the Revolution

Acknowledgements

There are so many to thank. I couldn't have gotten here without the many people who have helped me and guided me over the years.

To my brother and coach Garrett J. White: Thank you for showing me how to sit in the darkness and light the divine fire within. Thank you for the countless hours of coaching, conversation, and encouragement. You were there for me for many years before Warrior and I am honored to have been one of the first in the Brotherhood of Warriors.

To my brother and mentor, C-Baugh (Casey), who got me out of the darkness during those crucial years of rebuilding: Thank you for recruiting me to do a job that put me back in the game. You helped me break paradigms of poverty to reveal possibilities for great prosperity. Thank you for believing in me.

To my brother and friend Shane Heath: Thank you for being a sounding board and a guide through many difficult and challenging times throughout my life. You've been a powerful spiritual mentor for me, and I thank you and honor you.

To Ashlee Raubach: Thank you for the photos. Thank you for capturing what I wanted for this project.

To Rob Secades: Thank you for the artwork and cover. Your work—like you—is outstanding.

To Sean McCool: Thank you for your final touches, which gave me clarity through this process, and thank you for your friendship.

To Ryan Stewman: Thank you for helping me to finish this book. It took me two years and multiple drafts, and you helped me knock it out in thirty days.

To my coach Dusan Djukich: Thank you for coaching me, guiding me, and inspiring me with your work, Straight-Line Leadership.

To my brother and coach Scott Byrd: Thank you for being a powerful mentor and helping me see endless possibilities in life when I began as a coach. The work we did together has laid an enormous foundation for who I am today.

To Lisa Giles: Thank you for helping to piece my thoughts together, and for making this flow smoothly and powerfully.

To Michael and Jenny: This doesn't exist without you and I am forever grateful for the endless edits, revisions, and your extreme patience with me. We have more projects in front of us and more mountains to climb together and I look forward to it. Thank you.

To Sweetie Berry: Our work has just begun and you have been instrumental in helping me see possibilities with this project. Thank you for holding space in our calls together to help me see what I could not see.

To Nicholas Neilson: Thank you for your finishing touches to the book and powerful insights to the work in front of us. "The Revolution has Begun."

To my clients, who teach me valuable lessons along the way as I help you to see possibilities in your own lives: I honor each one of you who chooses to create and commit to the impossible.

To my parents: Royal and Alameda West, Setema and Tory Gali, thank you. Language could not possibly express my love, appreciation, gratitude and endless thanks for how you raised me, the life you gave me and the example and support you have been to me and my little family as I've journeyed through life.

To my sons, I love you. You truly are Divine Warrior Kings who can create anything you want for your life. You inspire me to be my best.

To my Love, I LOVE YOU. Thank you believing in me when I forgot who I was along the way. You are the best thing that's ever happened to me. Through all the ups and downs, you've been a perfect display of real power. When did you fall in love with hip hop?

CHAPTER 1

Crossing the Ocean

| ı ı ı ı ı | ı ı ı ı ı | ı ı ı ı ı | ı ı ı ı ı | ı ı ı ı ı | ı ı ı ı ı | ı ı ı ı

"Live. Love. Learn. Leave a legacy."
—Stephen Covey

I was in disbelief. We were packing up our home, the home we had lived in for nearly four years. I had lived in Utah for thirty-five years, and now I was moving my wife, our kids, and our few belongings to Orange County, California.

Those thirty-five years contained the highest and lowest points in my life. I had gone from winning the Super Bowl to selling my championship ring to put food on the table and gas in the car. My wife stood by me as I fought through extreme self-doubt and financial insecurity, and rejoiced with me when I surmounted those obstacles and reinvented myself again and again.

Now the dark days were distant, and I was ready to take another leap of faith.

A big part of me was excited to follow my dream of inspiring others to live powerfully, but another part of me was anxious. Sometimes doubt would creep in and I'd ask myself, *Can I do this? Can I move two states away, a thousand-plus miles from home, and make it?*

The answer was yes. I knew it would be OK.

How did I know? I knew because a great man had done the same thing sixty years earlier. He didn't cross two states and a thousand miles, however; he crossed the Pacific Ocean and traveled over six thousand miles to the foreign land that would become his new home.

That man was my father.

As a young boy, my father had worked in the taro patches on the islands of Samoa. Every single week, he'd see a cargo plane in the sky and say, "Mom, I want to be on that plane!" His mom would glance up at him briefly before returning to her work. Many people had dreams of leaving the island. Few ever did. And yet, again and again he would say, "Mom, I want to be on that plane!"

After weeks and weeks of listening to him tell her that he wanted to be on that plane, his mother looked at him and said, "If you want to be on that plane, you have to do well with a pencil and paper." She was talking about school.

My father had heard of a Mormon school in Samoa that taught English and allowed their students to wear pants instead of the traditional *lavalava,* which is a rectangular cloth worn as a wrap to cover one's body. The name of that school was Pesega, and it became his way to cross the ocean.

My father found the Mormon missionaries, got baptized, and studied hard in order to score high enough on his exams to get into the school. Come what may, he would realize his dreams, no matter how distant they seemed—dreams that focused on a tiny, moving dot miles up in the sky.

| | | | |

Samoa was a third-world country, and that plane signified the promise of a faraway land where my father could live a good life. Even though he had never left the country, he knew there was a possibility of something better for his family. He didn't speak English, but he knew he wanted to go to the States when a visiting interpreter told him that the streets of America were paved with gold and money grew on trees. That plane was his ticket to opportunity.

My father knew that education could take him to a new country where there was running water—a country filled with refrigerators, cars, planes—and most of all, possibility. He wanted a land of promise where he could thrive and grow as a man, as a husband, and as a father. He wanted to make his mother proud and to live that better life he had heard about.

Not only did he get into the Mormon school, he also went on to earn a scholarship to the Church College of Hawaii. He went from working in a taro patch to receiving a higher education in America. My father had achieved first big goal; he had "arrived."

My father cried when he left his homeland, but he was determined, and unwilling to settle for the life Samoa offered him. He'd actualized a vision to create greater opportunity for himself and his future family. Even when we accomplish our goals in life and move up in the world, the pain of leaving what's comfortable can bring tears … but it can also serve to remind us how far we have come.

When my father arrived in Hawaii, he slept in a bed for the first time in his life. Imagine having never seen a bed before and having no idea what to do with it! He took the few supplies he'd brought from Samoa, placed them on the bed, and slept on the floor. It would take some time for him to get used to this strange place.

While living in Hawaii, my father got a job and sent money back to his mother as often as he made it. He met a beautiful young lady and they got married. Shortly afterward, they had their first child, a baby girl. He dropped out of school because he realized he could make more money driving a taxi, performing in traditional dances at the hotels in Waikiki, and working whatever side-hustles he could find there.

After years of shifting from one job to another, struggling to make ends meet and support his growing family, my father decided to leave Hawaii to be closer to family members on the mainland. He had relatives in Missouri, and it was there that he had hopes of finding more opportunities. He gathered his family together and crossed the ocean. The rest of the story … well, that's still to come.

| | | | |

My father had a goal of creating a better life for his family. Once in Missouri, he brought many of his siblings over from the Samoan islands, helping them to get started in the States. By doing this, he showed his family how to live life in the service of others and what's possible when one is sincerely committed to the impossible. His vision and tenacity have always inspired me.

My mom and dad sacrificed so much to give us a better life, and they gave us much more than that. I watched them work job after job because they had a vision for their children's future. My parents' generation believed in hard work, persistence, and the will to do whatever is necessary. I now know what they knew—and perhaps you do too: The impact of a parent's legacy is felt deep in the hearts and souls of their children.

I look at my three boys today and I know that if I do not honor my commitments, my boys may fall into a path of irresponsibility, mediocrity and carelessness. I do not want this. I don't want my sons looking at me saying, "I never want to be like him." Instead, I want my sons to look at me and say, "I know all things are possible; just look at what my dad has done. He is my hero."

Create a Life of Significance

In ancient Christian Scriptures, men and women were told of the Promised Land, a place reserved for the chosen people. These people had visions of a greater opportunity, so they traveled to find it, just as my father and mother did. I teach my sons to do the same.

Every single day I ask my boys, "Who's in charge of your life?"

They repeat back to me, "I am."

Then I ask them, "Who's got it better than us?"

They yell, "Nobody!"

I love and honor my parents deeply. They showed me what was possible. They showed me that when a man is dedicated to providing for himself, his wife, and his children, he can wake up every single day, put his shoulder to the wheel, and do the required work to get the desired results.

I have a duty not only to teach my sons, but also to live what I teach. I have a responsibility to show them what's possible and how to turn the impossible into a reality—not merely by what I say, but by the way I live, what I do, and who I am. They have to be able to feel it through how I treat them and how I speak to them.

It takes courage to leave your comfort zone and journey somewhere you've never been before, doing things you've never done. It's difficult leaving what is familiar, making the big leap to leave home, learning a new language, and going to a place where you could face serious discrimination—a place where there are no guarantees and no free lunches.

It takes courage to live your vision—write that book, start that business, make that phone call, try out for the team, or ask that person out on a date. It takes bravery to write and sing a song, to create art, or to ask for a promotion. It takes boldness to take your cell phone and shoot a video selfie for Facebook or upload your message to Snapchat.

If you're going to create a life of real, radical results, a life that you love, a life of significance, *you've got to choose courage over fear.*

My mother did. My father did. They still do to this day. If you want to create a life that you can be proud of, you'll have many opportunities to choose courage, and you *must* choose it.

My parents did for me what I've been doing for my sons. My mom and dad worked countless hours—graveyard shifts, swing shifts, and multiple jobs. They taught me that if you want something, you go get it. If you want something, you set a goal and you work your butt off to make it happen. They taught me … but more important, they *showed* me by their example. My parents are paragons of courage, faith, and hard work.

Millions of immigrants travel and sacrifice everything they have to get to a land that offers greater opportunity. If they can do it, certainly *you* can. **There's no reason that you can't "cross the ocean" right now in your own life.**

That can mean different things for different people. It could mean committing to a workout routine in order to weaponize your body, even though you haven't exercised in years. It could mean listening to that voice within that says, *It's time to write that book.* It could mean starting a new business or finally having the courage to confront a problem you've been avoiding.

"Crossing the ocean" may mean having the courage to walk away from a marriage that hasn't been working for years and which has actually begun to damage the children. On the flip side, it might mean confronting a relationship that has gone stale, and fighting for it.

The number of funerals I attend increases as I grow older. At every one of these funerals, my mind wanders to my own funeral at some point down the road, and I ask myself, *Am I actualizing who I need to be and acting the way I want to act to bring about the results I truly desire?*

It was this very question that led me to make that move to Orange County all those years ago. On that last day in Utah, just before taking the leap, I thought of my father crossing thousands upon thousands of miles of ocean to come to America. Surely if he could do it, I, too, could make the move away from my family, out of my comfort zone, and far from all that I had ever known. Surely I could come to Orange County and not only get by, but thrive, prosper, and dominate in my profession.

Orange County represented a "leveling up" in my perspective as well as in my physical surroundings. You can't fake production as a businessman in Orange County. You can't pretend that all is well when behind closed doors, the whole enterprise is going up in flames. People see the smoke. You either produce or get out. And I was ready for anything. I was ready to choose courage over fear. I was ready to cross my ocean.

One of my coaches said something to me that I've never forgotten: "If you knew how short life really is, and that in a matter of weeks, days, or hours, your body could be a pile of bones in the ground six feet under, you'd make bigger requests and you'd stop playing small. You wouldn't be afraid to ask for anything."

There are no guarantees in life. You're sitting there reading this book right now, but in a matter of hours, your time could come. So ask yourself, *What do I really want to create for my life, my spouse, my family, and my legacy? How do I really want to be remembered?*

I invite you with all my heart to take a good, honest look at your life today and start asking the difficult questions. You will find these questions at the end of the chapter, and throughout the book as well. Grab your journal and do the work. This journey will demand reflection and introspection. By really questioning what you want and what you're doing, you will find the path that is right for you.

It is all too easy to avoid the difficult questions. It takes strength to confront and ask and get to the heart of what really matters, but doing so is the only path to achieving your goals. Regardless of your background, your religion, or the color of your skin, wake up, turn on your brain, and declare that you're "crossing the ocean," just as my father did.

Questions to Consider Carefully and Answer:

- What is your vision for your life?
- What is your ocean to cross? What prevents you from getting there?
- How will you know you have arrived?
- What would it take for you to open up your mind and heart to dream again?

CHAPTER 2

Weak Body, Strong Dreams
The Power of Clarity to Create Change

|ıııı|ıııı|ıııı|ıııı|ıııı|ıııı|ıııı

"No one has ever drowned in sweat."
—Lou Holtz

I t was 2002, and I was lifting weights in the new weight room at Gillette Stadium. The facilities were clean and beautiful. We were fresh off a Super Bowl championship, and headquarters was buzzing with excitement and anticipation of the next year. I was working out next to another Samoan player named Ula Tuitele, out of Colorado State. I was bench-pressing and struggling to get one rep. As I wrestled with the rep, the strength coach, Mike Woicik, walked up and gave me a look that said, *Are you serious?*

Aloud, he said to the both of us, "You are the weakest Samoans I've ever trained in my life." He was grinning, kind of joking, but also serious.

We laughed with him and I replied, "I may be one of the weakest, but dude, I'm definitely one of the better-looking ones, for sure." Yes, I was serious. I may not have been the strongest or the fastest, but I knew I had an edge. All kidding aside, it wasn't my looks that gave me an edge. Not by a long shot. It was my desire to outwork others and chase my dreams. My mind-set was the key—and had been ever since I was a kid.

When I was in kindergarten, my dad coached our flag football team. My older brother and cousin were great. They were fast, strong, and athletic. But I was just a part of the team—the snot-nosed kid who was the coach's son. I was taller and bigger than most kids, but my body was uncoordinated. I wasn't very good at sports because I wasn't very fast or strong.

Then my parents divorced. They had seven kids to raise, so I didn't get the opportunity to continue playing a lot of organized sports. We lived in Provo, Utah, and my dad and I used to watch Brigham Young University football games together. The game resonated with me, and I wanted to play. I could see myself on the field at LaVell Edwards Stadium, with the "Y" football helmet on, waving to the crowd. My fantasy seemed to be in the "impossible" category because of my lack of speed and strength, but the *drive* in me was deep enough to motivate me to figure out how to make it happen.

Middle school opened up my world. When I entered seventh grade, I got my first opportunity to play tackle football at school. I thought, *This is it—junior high. I get to play tackle football. I can't wait to play!* I acquired my shoulder pads, my pants, my jersey, and my helmet. I had visions of dominating and crushing my opponents. I was jubilant and ready to become a football star.

I was also in for a rude awakening.

The first day of practice, I threw up and passed out. It was hard, because I had never really challenged my body like that before. Envisioning myself working hard was very different from *physically* working hard. I actually wanted to quit that first day. I was unprepared for what was required to become a great athlete. I hated football for the remainder of seventh grade. I detested going to practice because we had to run so much. As a Polynesian kid, long-distance running, sprints, and conditioning weren't my thing. I was always at the end of the pack during running drills. I loathed going to practice so much that I'd wish for rain and thunderstorms, which would cancel it. I also hated playing the games. But I especially hated that I wasn't a good player. Every game was nerve-racking, and I would pray to *God, Please don't let them put me in, God. Please, oh, please.* That's how much I disliked the game early on. We rarely enjoy that which we feel unprepared to accomplish well.

Maybe there was a time in your life when *you* felt like quitting. Here's the good news: If you feel like quitting, you're doing something right. It means you're pushing and expanding. If you haven't wanted to quit something, then you're not pushing hard enough.

There are a lot of things I've wanted to quit. I wanted to quit football, but I kept going because I never wanted that to define me. I made up my mind at a pretty early age that I would not give up on myself. It was a very slow and difficult start, but in time, my will to work would start to pay off. By the time I got to eighth grade, I still wasn't very athletic, but I was OK—although there were several kids who were far better athletes than I. I had something most of my teammates didn't have, however; I had determination.

Focus on the Goals

By the time I got to ninth grade, I had grown four inches since the previous season. I was now tall and lanky, although I still wasn't very strong or fast. My physical growth did not help me with the athleticism needed for the gridiron (in fact, my future success as a player would have little to do with my physical ability). I looked for every edge to be better, but there was no indication that I would improve. When I started my sophomore year, I was barely 170 pounds, which by today's standards is not very big at all, especially for the position of defensive end.

I began to write down my goals in a red journal. I looked at them every single day. My goals were simple: I wanted to win a state championship. I wanted to get a scholarship to play football at BYU. And I wanted more than anything to be the best player in the state.

I finished my sophomore year in the fall of 1991. At the end of the football season, Bryce Monsen, the varsity head football coach, gave a speech. I can't remember the exact words he said, but I will never forget how I felt. Every day I looked at the goals I'd written in my red journal, but nothing seemed to change—until that day. Coach Monsen helped me to visualize what it would be like to achieve my goals. He taught me that taking action was the only way to make desires become reality.

I decided that the first step on my road to BYU would be to become a starter the next year in high school. I aspired to be "the man." I knew I would have to outwork everyone. (This mentality, this determination always to outwork everyone, would become a key component of the success I would achieve later in my life.) At that moment, in the late fall of 1991, I made a commitment to myself that I was going to be a starter in my junior year.

Now that I'd set that goal, I needed a plan of action. That plan consisted of eating like a horse at every meal and lifting weights four days a week without exception. This was the pivotal year when I began develop a love affair with the weight room. Randall Murray, a good friend of mine and our middle linebacker, lifted weights with me. We went from lifting together at Mountain View High School to lifting at World Gym in Provo.

Every Monday, Tuesday, Thursday, and Friday, we were there. Just as my father and my mother had set goals to make a better life for themselves and for their family, now I had a goal—and I was willing to pay the price for it. In fact, I loved paying the price.

My friends asked me why I wasn't trying out for basketball that year. I knew that if I played basketball, I wouldn't be able to lift weights and get stronger. If I didn't get stronger, I wasn't sure I could become a starter my junior year. So day after day, I worked out: chest, back, triceps, legs, squats, clings, curls, pull-ups, sit-ups, crunches. You name it, and I did it.

I soon noticed changes in my body. I wanted to watch my progress, so I'd look in the mirror and flex every day. I looked at my reflection in the shiny surface of our refrigerator. I gazed at myself as I walked past mirrors, and slept with my shirt off so that my focus was always on my body. That's no exaggeration; I was obsessed with becoming bigger, faster, and stronger.

And bigger, faster, and stronger I became. Between my sophomore and junior years, I put on thirty-five pounds. By the time I reached my final height of six-foot-four, I had muscles popping out of my clothes. I went into my junior year weighing 205 pounds. One of the great benefits of working out is the confidence it builds, and mine was through the roof.

"Obsessed" is a word that less dedicated people use to describe those who are committed to their goals. I was obsessed that year with lifting and eating in order to get stronger so I could be the starter in my junior year. I often thought about what that would entail. I visualized myself getting sacks, making tackles, and being a poster boy. I wasn't the poster boy in high school, but I would be by my senior year at BYU.

If you're going to have any type of high-level success, you need to engage focus and be obsessed. Kobe Bryant was obsessed with winning. So was Michael Jordan. Tom Brady is obsessed with being the G.O.A.T. (greatest of all time). A highly successful person is obsessed with learning the skills and practices to win, and does whatever it takes.

When you begin to invest time, energy, and resources in your goals, your confidence grows. Asking the right questions keeps you on track. Every day I asked myself, *What have I done today to win a state championship?* I was possessed and obsessed. I wanted to win state. Having goals and targets motivated me. Having an end in mind dictated how I behaved. Even if I didn't like doing the required work sometimes, desiring the outcome and committing to it made the grind and hustle irrelevant.

Ask yourself the hard questions daily: *What have I done today to ensure that I win in my life? What am I doing today to ensure that my marriage, family, and business are winning and becoming exactly what I want them to become?*

Your body can either be a weapon or an anchor. It will give you energy or it will take energy. Regardless of where you are physically, give your body the gift of exercise, movement, and sweat. The habit of banging and clanging weights became one of the greatest contributors to my success, and I still do it today. You always perform better when your confidence is at its highest level, and physical fitness can be the greatest confidence booster.

I recognized at an early age that I wouldn't ever be really, *really* strong, but my body could pass the look test. My biceps, chest, shoulders, calves, and quads could pop, and I'd have a confidence I could take with me onto the practice field and into the game. There's something different about people who work out. They take on life with a sense of invincibility. They deal with adversity and stress differently than people who have never worked out and who don't know how to challenge their bodies. Moving your muscles has so many benefits in addition to allowing you to gain strength. It allows the body to release stress, change its internal chemistry, and release sweat and toxins. It's a function of a healthy body to use every muscle.

Do you have to lift weights to have good health? Not necessarily. There are other options, including yoga, Pilates, running, swimming, biking, hiking, push-ups, and pull-ups. I've done all of these. The point is, *move your body and push yourself consistently.*

I ask myself daily, *Did you sweat today? Did you weaponize your body? Did you move your body in a way that pushed its capacity?* Fitness and nutrition must be a huge part of life for someone who wants a life of radical results—a life one can love.

I'm so grateful that my varsity head coach challenged us that day, because since then, working out has been a normal part of my regimen. And after that day, I went on to achieve my goals: I became a starter and then I went on to play at BYU.

At BYU, it was no different. I never missed workouts. I loved the weight room. I loved how I felt. I skipped road trips because I didn't want to miss my workouts. I passed on trips to Lake Powell because I refused to miss a day in the weight room. That dedication and goal setting took me from begging to be sidelined as a seventh grader to playing pro ball in the NFL. And in the transition from BYU to the NFL, I took the same approach. I worked hard in the weight room and put on twenty pounds in preparation for the league. I was barely 265 pounds when I left BYU. A year later, I was 285 pounds with a lean 12 percent body fat.

Are you willing to pay the price for what you want? Have you written down goals that you look at every single day?

These are the goals that I first wrote down in my journal:

- Be a starter and All-State at Mountain View
- Be an All-American at Mountain View
- Get a scholarship to BYU
- Serve a two-year mission for my church

I still have that red journal from high school, and I still look at it often with fondness and gratitude that someone inspired me to write down my goals and my plan for achieving them. None of these questions or goals matter if you cannot tell the truth. Be real about where you are, what you want, and what's required to get there.

Once you tell the truth, the formula below will help you to achieve the exact results you want in your life. The formula works. It's the formula I used in high school to put weight on, to be an All-State athlete, to get a scholarship, and eventually to become a two-year starter at BYU and an All-Conference player. It's the formula I used to get into the NFL, to learn to play the piano, and to make an abundance of money in my businesses. I still use this formula today, and I offer it to you.

Here's the formula:

1. **DECLARE**
2. **DEFINE**
3. **DECIDE**
4. **COMMIT**
5. **STOP STOPPING**

These specific words were given to me by Dusan Djukich, author of *Straight-Line Leadership*. While I didn't use these exact words growing up, my principles and processes were the same.

DECLARE What You Want

Throughout these first two chapters, I've asked a host of questions for clarity. Tony Robbins said, "Clarity is power," and it's true. When you know what you want and why you want it, you've begun the journey. The only way to get what you want is to first *know* what you want. So what do *you* want for your life?

So many people are afraid to declare what they want. They are afraid they may not get it, so they keep it bottled up inside. Don't do that! Life is short, remember? It's certainly too short to watch other people play the game of life while you sit in the stands and watch. It is too short not to go after what you want or do what you feel you were born to do. It's too short to be mediocre, or even to settle for "good." Why not be the best possible you?

What do you want and why does that matter? Declare and write down the answers to these questions now. Doing so will give you perspective and power.

DEFINE the Actions That Would Bring You Your Desired Results

I call these "NRAs"—Necessary Required Actions.

This is where many people fail. They get some form of clarity and then they never sit down and define the skills and systems that are required for them to reach their goals. To succeed as a skilled player in football, I had to gain weight, increase my strength and speed, and increase my football IQ. So I did.

What's required to go make the money you want to make?

What's required to increase love, passion, communication, and intimacy in your marriage?

What's required for you to get what you want in your life?

What core competencies must be developed?

What stories must you believe about yourself to help you get what you want?

Once you define your NRAs, you're ready for the next step. If you have a goal, a target, or an outcome, and you haven't defined what's required to achieve it, you're wasting your time if you're simply looking at your vision board and trying to "attract" it to you.

DECIDE Whether or Not You're Willing to Perform the NRAs

This is a simple and very necessary step. It's one thing to declare what you want to create for your life; it's another to define the NRAs. You have to ask yourself, *Am I going to do what's required?* I also refer to this as "paying the price" or "paying the piper." Every prize in life has a price attached to it. If you pay the price, you get the prize. If you don't pay the price, you don't get the prize.

There's a price required to have a great marriage. That price and the NRAs might be:

- Consistent daily messages of love, honor, and appreciation
- Consistent weekly date nights
- Being present (phones off and completely focused on your spouse)
- Finding and creating ways to serve your spouse consistently
- Improving your communication and listening skills
- Improving your skills in intimacy, touch, and love

There's a price required to have a booming business that keeps the bank accounts full. That price and the NRAs might be:

- Becoming more competent in the necessary skills
- Mastering leadership
- Mastering the sales process to convert those leads to cash and happy customers
- Implementing systems and processes to streamline everything
- Building the team and culture
- Investing time, energy, and money consistently into your team, employees, systems, assets, technology, etc.

I say to my sons daily, "You can have anything in life if you…?" And they respond, "PAY THE PRICE!" It's true: Once you decide that you're willing to pay that price for the desired prize, and that you're going to perform the necessary required actions to create what you want, you're on to the next step.

COMMIT to the Outcome

Commitment is defined by three things:

1. Knowing and doing what is required to get the intended results
2. Doing what you said you would do to get the intended results
3. Acting decisively, in spite of unwanted thoughts, feelings, emotions and moods to get the intended results

Can you commit to performing the NRAs and paying the price? If you can, you'll get the results you want. I'm not asking you to do your best, or to do all you know. I'm telling you to "do what's required," and without a doubt, you'll get the results you desire.

When a client asks or complains about not getting a result, I ask three questions:

1. Did you do what was required?
2. Did you do the things you said you would do to get the result?
3. Did you take decisive action in spite of any unwanted thoughts, feelings, emotions, or moods?

Once you've committed, you're ready for the final step of the formula.

STOP STOPPING

The business world is filled with people who have "stopped." Now, if you're doing the wrong actions—i.e., things that don't move you closer to what you want—you should absolutely stop. But when you're engaged in the right actions and paying that price, stop stopping. Don't give up when it gets hard. Train yourself to keep going.

From the weight room in high school to the field at BYU to the NFL, I kept going. And for you, my friend, to produce and create a life that you love and to live your greatest version of yourself, you must learn to stop stopping. Inevitably, if you stop stopping, you'll always reach your desired destination. Always. Those who repeatedly quit never win, and repeatedly quitting is not how powerful people play. The next time you're tempted to stop, go back to why you started. Think about your *WHY*. Remember what you committed to and keep that commitment. You'll be happy you did.

Questions to Consider Carefully and Answer:

- Do you have goals for your life?
- How often do you write them down and look at them?
- Have you defined what's necessary to achieve those goals?
- Are you willing to do those NRAs for your goals?
- Why do you want what you say you want?
- Do you want it only if it's easy, or no matter what?
- Are your goals a MUST, or just a "would be nice if I got them?"
- Are you willing to pay the price for your prize and promised lands?

CHAPTER 3

Wounded but Healing
Lessons in Selfless Love and Loving Self

| ι ι ι ι ι | ι ι ι ι ι | ι ι ι ι ι | ι ι ι ι ι | ι ι ι ι ι | ι ι ι ι ι | ι ι ι ι ι

*"The best way to find yourself is to
lose yourself in the service of others."*
—Mahatma Gandhi

The sun pounded my face and the humidity forced sweat out of my body as if I were sitting in a sauna while wrapped in towels. We had been cruising the Pacific Ocean for almost two hours in a tiny boat with a hand-steered engine when the driver stopped the boat and said, "Get out and walk. The tide is too low."

I was wearing a nice white shirt, tie, dress slacks, and dress shoes, and carrying a suitcase. So I took off my shoes and socks, stuffed them into my bag, rolled up my slacks, and stepped out of the tiny little boat and onto the coral. The water came to just over my knees. It was about forty yards to the shoreline. I was lucky in that I didn't cut up my feet while walking to shore. There must have been angels around me.

21

Once I got to the shoreline, my companion looked at me with a grin. Elder Hawkins also had on a dress shirt, now yellowed after months in the tropical sun. Instead of slacks, he wore beat-up khakis.

"Are you ready?" he asked.

For the next twenty-five minutes, we climbed a steep trail on the side of the mountain to get to our "house," which was a twelve-by-twelve-foot plywood box covered with tin. The rain would hit the tin and run into a little rain gutter that dripped into a water tank. From there, a PVC pipe ran from the water tank into the home, and that's how we got our water. We drank rainwater fresh off the roof. There was no electricity, no plumbing, and—you guessed it—no running water. This was what I'd left my home and my family and taken two years off from school and football for. And it would be home, sweet home for the next two years of my life.

It had all started back in junior high. My self-esteem was extremely low in the seventh and eighth grade. I didn't like myself very much, and I definitely didn't love myself like I do today. I didn't feel I fit in. I wore the same pair of jeans the entire year. It wasn't that my parents didn't love us; they just had so many kids that it was hard to provide an expansive wardrobe for all of them. I was bouncing back and forth between my dad's place and my mom's place because of my parents' divorce a few years earlier. My confidence was so low that I wouldn't have been able to look a girl in the eyes if my life had depended on it.

At that time, all the kids had designer clothes and expensive shoes (Air Jordans had just hit the market). I began to notice that my family wasn't wealthy, and it affected the way I viewed myself. In *your* life, has there been a time for you when you didn't see yourself as powerful, worthy, or successful? That's where I was. (But that's OK; this story has a great ending. Keep reading!)

I wasn't very good in sports yet, and I didn't have the confidence that I believed most of my peers had. But everything changed in ninth grade.

I moved up to my dad's in Orem, Utah, and began attending seminary that year, as is customary for young Latter-day Saints. I was the new kid on the block, with an extra four inches added to my height. And I was finally starting to come into my own in football. The following years would be life-changing.

A Life of Purpose

I grew up as a member of the Church of Jesus Christ of Latter-day Saints, also known as the Mormon Church. I was baptized at the age of eight, and I went to church on Sundays. At that point in my life, I really didn't know if the church was right for me. I accepted my religion because it was what I had been taught by my parents. I prayed to God, but not always sincerely—more out of habit and culture. I'd read the Scriptures, but not consistently, and certainly not every day.

I walked into seminary on the first day of ninth grade and sat down. All I could think about at the time was football. As I took my seat in the classroom on that hot September day, my seminary teacher, Craig Ostler, stood up in front of the class.

After our opening prayer to start seminary, he held up the Book of Mormon and asked, "How many of you know this book is true?"

I'd never even thought about it. It was what I had been taught to believe, so I kind of assumed it to be true. But something was different about this day. The question struck me in a way I'd never felt before. Something touched my heart as he asked the question again: "How many of you know this is true?" For the first time in my life, I couldn't say that I really knew that it *was* true. Sure, I attended church. I went to activities for the youth. I did all the church things because mom and dad said, "This is what we do." But I didn't know for myself. God touched my heart that day, and I began a journey that would shape my entire life.

As he continued his lesson, my teacher promised us two things that day: "If you read the Scriptures every day, and if you pray every day, you will come to know the truth of these things, and God will pour blessings into your life."

Sure enough, I began to find the truth that year in ninth grade. In 1990, I began to read the Book of Mormon every day. It was difficult at first; the language is tough because it's a different type of English. I also began to pray. We lived in a tiny home with six boys and one girl, so there wasn't a lot of privacy, but I would always find a way to get on my knees and pray to God. I began to pray as I walked to school every morning. When I went to football practice, I prayed and looked to the mountains as I conversed with God. I would ask God, *Please bless me and help me. Give me strength and help me to remember my assignments on the field.* I became a praying, God-fearing man. I understood what it meant to "pray always."

Prayer, Scripture study, and sincere church attendance would completely alter the landscape of my spiritual and personal life. At the end of my ninth-grade year, I knew for myself that God was real, that He answers prayers, that He loves His children, and that the Book of Mormon was true. That one year radically affected my life, and I looked at the world through a new lens. God required specific things from us as His children, and He's asked us to avoid specific things. One thing He requires is our service. I would go on to read the Book of Mormon another seven times before I would board an airplane headed to Guam, and from there to Chuuk State in Micronesia to serve my two-year mission.

Throughout high school I read and quoted the Scriptures. It became a way of living for me. I knew who God was for me, and it changed me. I began to love people and forgive more easily. I became a peacemaker. I loved the gospel of Jesus Christ, and I loved the fruits of the Scriptures, the Old Testament, the New Testament, the Book of Mormon, and the

Doctrine and Covenants. I loved knowing that God loved me and had a plan for me. I loved how I felt about myself.

By the time my senior year of high school arrived, my beliefs were strong. I knew the truths of the gospel. I knew the truths of the Scriptures, and I knew God had a plan for me. Knowing my life had a plan gave me the confidence I needed to go and be all I could be.

A Scripture that gave me immense power and hope is found in Proverbs 3:5–6:

Trust in the LORD with all thine heart; and lean not unto thine own understanding.

In all thy ways acknowledge him, and he shall direct thy paths.

I began to trust God. I began to really lean on Him and to do all I could to stay worthy of guidance from the Spirit of God. All of this made it very easy to go on a mission. I knew that I had this incredible amount of joy in my life, and I wanted other people to experience it. I wanted people to experience the Spirit of God speaking to them as it had spoken to me.

Before going out to the mission field, I was fired up about teaching people something that had brought me immense joy. I was convinced I would baptize everyone out there. Upon arriving and seeing our ramshackle hut, I realized that our mission would not be easy.

My first night in Chuuk was not pleasant. We slept on futons. I woke up to a trail of ants carrying a dead insect right past my face. They just moved along right in front of me as if I weren't there. Since there was no running water, I took a bucket shower while mosquitoes bit me left and right. I couldn't stop sweating. I was miserable. I pretended to be happy, but this was not what I'd thought I would be getting into. I was homesick.

Learning a Foreign Language

I had to adapt to the island, and that meant I needed to learn the language as fast as I could so I could teach the people. The beautiful part about serving a mission is that when you go in with the right attitude, learning becomes a journey. I had no idea what these people were saying. I couldn't speak or understand the language; it just sounded like crazy noises. The only person on the island other than me who spoke English was my companion.

Every night I would pray and ask God to bless me and help me to learn the language so I could teach people. I did what I had done before: learn, practice, study, and memorize. I felt inadequate in my calling as a representative of Jesus Christ. I literally cried every morning and night in prayer for help to love the locals and learn their language. I took every opportunity I had to speak to people. I began to serve them. I began to teach them about Jesus Christ and tell them that God had a plan for them. I began to develop a selfless love and a way of living to bring others to Jesus Christ. I began to lose myself in the work. I never stopped talking with the kids, and I would mimic their speech. Eventually, it started coming together.

In serving others, we come to love others. If you want to love your wife or your children more, serve them. Make them breakfast, help them with work, perform acts of kindness, and give time to them. Whomever you serve is whom you love. I loved these people because I was serving them daily.

Whom are you serving consistently?

Within two months, I became fluent in the Chuukese language. By three months, I was dreaming in the language and speaking like an islander. I was teaching the wonderful people of Chuuk. I had grown up hearing the expression, "Whom God calls, God qualifies," and now I was on His errand and His time. I knew my abilities and capacities had been strengthened. My command of the language was so solid that I thought, *I'm going to be one of those guys who lives here for two years, and people will think that I'm from here.*

Five months into that first mission in Faichuuk, Chuuk, I got the radio call that said I was being transferred to Guam. I couldn't believe it. I had spent five months learning this language, teaching and serving the people on this tiny little island, and now I was headed back to Guam.

A week later I got on a plane, flew back to Guam, and opened up a new area on the south tip of Guam called Merizo. Over the next eighteen months, I traveled all over Micronesia—to Palau, Yap, Saipan, Pohnpei, Kosrae, Ebeye, and the Marshall Islands. I met and trained missionaries in all of these places. Leadership became a part of my everyday life. I encouraged our missionaries to work harder and smarter, and to be obedient to mission rules. I was helping them to live the truths of the gospel of Jesus Christ. Throughout this time, I continued to hear the whisperings of the Spirit, or what I often refer to as the "voice."

We All Have a Mission

I was literally on a mission. You're on a mission too. What is your mission in life? The more you view your life as a mission, rather than a series of random, spontaneous events, the more powerfully you act to achieve greatness. Your beliefs always lead to your behaviors, which always lead to your results. My spiritual beliefs shaped and forged my personal prayer and Scripture studies in ninth grade. Those truths shifted the way I viewed my life; I viewed myself now as a son of the Almighty God. I viewed my role in the world as that of a contributor, and not just a taker. I saw myself as being able to make a difference in the lives of others.

I came home after the two-year mission, and things began changing rapidly. I had loved my mission. I'd loved the people who didn't have very much. Today, we have smart phones, e-mail, social media, and countless other distractions. The people of Chuuk, on the other hand, live simple lives. They live off the land. They fish, farm, and enjoy one another's company. I sometimes wonder if they are better off than we are. It reminds me of a story I read many years later in a sandwich shop.

This is the story that started the "be more with less" movement for me after I left football. While I knew "all work and no play" wasn't the way, I thought I would forever be stuck in the cycle of working to live. I thought I would forever have car payments and credit card debt, and never have enough money at the end of the month. This story is my inspiration to slow down, reassess, and get real about how I want to live life:

An American investment banker was at the pier of a small coastal Mexican village when a small boat with just one fisherman docked. Inside the small boat were several large yellowfin tuna. The American complimented the Mexican fisherman on the quality of his fish and asked how long it had taken to catch them.

The fisherman replied, "Only a little while."

The American then asked him why he hadn't stayed out longer to catch more fish. The fisherman replied that he had enough to support his family's immediate needs.

The American asked, "But what do you do with the rest of your time?"

The Mexican fisherman said, "I sleep late, fish a little, play with my children, take siestas with my wife, Maria, and stroll into the village each evening where I sip wine and play guitar with my amigos. I have a full and busy life."

The American scoffed, "I have an MBA from Harvard, and I can help you. You should spend more time fishing and buy a bigger boat with the proceeds. Then, with the proceeds from the bigger boat, you can buy several boats, and eventually, you can have a fleet of fishing boats. Instead of selling your catch to a middleman, you can sell directly to the processor, and eventually, you can open your own cannery. You can control the product, processing, and distribution. Of course, you will need to leave this small coastal fishing village and move to Mexico City, then L.A., and—eventually—New York City, where you can run your expanding enterprise."

The Mexican fisherman asked, "But how long would this all take?"

To which the American replied, "Fifteen to twenty years."

"But what then?" asked the fisherman.

The American laughed and said, "That's the best part. When the time is right, you can announce an IPO and sell your company stock to the public and become very rich. You will make millions!"

"Millions! Then what?"

The American said, "Then you'll retire and move to a small coastal fishing village where you will sleep late, fish a little, play with your kids, take siestas with your wife, and stroll to the village in the evenings where you can sip wine and play your guitar with your amigos."

—Anonymous

Remember what you're fighting for and why you're fighting for it. Prosperity is not just having financial abundance. True prosperity is living your greatest version of yourself. It is utilizing your natural gifts and developed talents for the benefit of others. Yes, an abundance of money can be that if you so desire and choose it.

Be wise as you pursue career goals and financial success. The last thing anyone ever wants is to get to the top of the ladder only to realize the ladder was leaning against the wrong wall. Get real about what prosperity would look like in your life so that you can enjoy the journey and celebrate when you achieve it.

Questions to Consider Carefully and Answer:

- Your beliefs dictate your behaviors, which produce your results. What are your beliefs in regard to:
    - Money and wealth?
    - Family and relationships?
    - Fitness and nutrition?
    - Spirituality and the purpose of life?
- What results will your current beliefs deliver?
- What skills must you learn in order to achieve your desired results?
- Whomever you serve is whom you love. Whom do you serve?

CHAPTER 4

Walking by Faith, Not by Sight
The Only Way to See Is to Go through It

| | | | | | | | | | | | | | | | | | | | | | | | | | | | | | | | | | | | | |

"Fate whispers to the warrior, 'You cannot withstand the storm.'
The warrior whispers back, 'I am the storm.'"
—Anonymous

I sat in the training room, confused and uncertain, wondering, *Am I supposed to play this game of football?* Football is a violent, highly competitive, dog-eat-dog, cutthroat game. It was a stark contrast to the two-year mission I'd been on, where all I did was pray, serve, love, attend church, and teach others the Gospel and Good Word. I'd lost the hunger to play football. Because of the two-year break I'd taken, my body was out of shape, which resulted in an injury early in the season. Now I was sitting in the training room, asking God, *What am I supposed to do with my life? What role do football and this college scholarship have in my life?*

Chad Lewis, a good friend of mine and one of the most positive guys you could ever meet, walked in and sat down next to me. He had finished up his time at BYU and was home from the NFL nursing an injury before heading back out. He went on to be All-Pro in the NFL. He asked me how I was doing, so I told him what I was struggling with and asked him what he thought I should do.

He said, "Let me ask you a question: What do you want to do with your life?"

I told him, "I want to have an impact on people. I want to make a difference. I want to lead, teach, coach, and inspire. I want to help people live the greatest lives possible."

He looked me straight in the eyes, with all the power and energy a man can have, and said, "Then you must succeed in the game of football. The only way you are going to inspire people with what God gave you is to kick butt on the field. You have to be a starter. You have to be on the posters. You have to be dominant so that people will want to hear from you and talk to you. Because when you are the best, people listen to you."

This was an answer to a prayer. I began looking at football not as a violent game, but as a vehicle, a tool to create more value for more people. Football gave me the platform to become a beacon of light to help men and women become whom they were supposed to be. Your job and your talents are opportunities to help other people if you are willing to "let your light so shine."[1]

God gave me an athletic physical body, and some talents and instincts to play football. Basketball? I was OK. Air hockey? I thought I was pretty good. But I really excelled on the field, coming off the edge like a race-car defensive end and knocking quarterbacks' heads off from their backside. Football was my game. And now it was more than my game; it was my gateway. You've got to focus on being the best in your field if you desire to lead others in theirs.

---

1   Matthew 5:16

Injuries and Adversity

My time at BYU was one of the craziest periods of growth in my life. I had shoulder surgery before my freshman season started. After my two-year mission, and over the following four years, I had four more surgeries, for a total of five. This challenged me to the very core. But I loved that I learned a lot about myself each time. One only learns through adversity. You discover a lot about yourself when you feel like you've given your best effort and it doesn't work out.

Fresh off my mission in 1997, the University of Washington destroyed us in our home opener. It was the first game of the season, and it wasn't even close. In the next game, we flew to Arizona and played ASU at the Sun Devil Stadium. I was running full speed on the first kickoff, playing special team, and the next thing I remember is waking up on the sideline with five minutes remaining in the first quarter. I had no idea where I was or what had happened. It was like a dream. I had no short-term memory. All of it was gone, and I looked around trying to figure out what was going on. My head was pounding and wouldn't stop ringing. I had a sharp pain in my right leg and I couldn't go back in because I couldn't find my helmet. I found out later that on the opening kickoff, I ran down the field and hit the blockers who were running full speed. Although I got up and ran off, my bell was rung. I was out of it for nearly twenty minutes on the sideline. One of the special team's players realized I was missing and that I had no idea what I was doing. As it turned out, I had suffered a deep concussion and a fractured leg. I had also injured my shoulder.

I missed a few games because of the fracture. These injuries were an indication of how committed I was and how badly I wanted to achieve my goals, no matter what. I wanted to be a starter. I wanted to be All-Conference. I wanted to be All-American. Of course, there was a part of me that wanted to play in the NFL and win big, to become an All-Pro Hall of Famer. I dream big. Do you?

Passing the Test

Adversity has a funny way of letting you know whether or not you really want the things you think you want. It tests your resolve and your willingness to do the required work. After my freshman year, I had another shoulder surgery. I came back in 1998—my sophomore year— as fierce as ever.

I was 250 pounds with less than 10 percent body fat. I could slam-dunk a basketball easily, and the coaches said I could run like a deer. I was in the best shape of my life. I conditioned hard that off-season and rehabbed consistently. Life was amazing. I thought, *This is my breakthrough year!* I was playing alongside guys like Chris Hoke, who had played for the Steelers for ten years, and Hans Olsen, who also had played in the NFL and could balance anything on his chin (seriously, *anything*). Byron Frisch was the end opposite me, and he looked like a man sketched out of a Marvel comic book. Behind us was linebacker Rob Morris, who ended up being a first-round draft pick for the Indianapolis Colts and a force on the defense.

We were going to play the University of Alabama in Tuscaloosa to start the season. I strained my right groin a week before the game. Then I strained my left groin because I had compensated so much in practice. As I continued to compensate, I strained my abs. I didn't practice at all that week, but I played in the Alabama game against Chris Samuels, a potential first-rounder in the NFL Draft. I didn't practice again the next week, and played in the Arizona State game. By the third game, against University of Washington, I couldn't move.

I was prepared, trained, and ready, and yet again, injuries struck. I missed a couple more games, once more testing my resolve and commitment. I continued to trust God and pray: "OK, Lord, I trust you. Let me just learn the lessons I need to learn, and if this is what I've got to do, so be it." At the end of that year, I had another shoulder surgery—my third in as many years.

By the time my junior year came around, I had earned my role as a starter. I couldn't work out as much that off-season because of my shoulder surgery, but I felt good coming into the season. I was quick and ready to dominate.

Again, I had learned a big lesson: **If you want something big, you will be tested in a big way.** Adversity will hit you. It's not even what happens to you that matters; it's what happens *within you* that counts. The stones of adversity can either bury you or become stepping-stones.

As a starting defensive end heading into my junior season, I set a goal of getting ten sacks that year. I made my plan and began visualizing it and working at it. Visualization is critical for high-level success. I envisioned myself exploding off the ball every play. I saw myself beating my opponent and then sacking the quarterback. My self-talk went like this: *I'm the fastest and quickest man on the planet. No one can block me. I'm too fast. I'm too quick.* I felt great about my approach to achieving that goal.

We beat University of Washington and Colorado State in our first two outings. We dropped a high-scoring shootout to the University of Virginia in our third game. I had zero sacks so far. I came close in those games, but hadn't put it together yet. In our fourth game against Cal Berkeley, it came together perfectly. The offense walked up to the line of scrimmage and I noticed the tendencies and formations. Then I exploded off the ball, executed one of my signature moves (which I had practiced thousands of times, mentally and physically), and I sacked the quarterback. Wow—it felt so good! Four games into the season, and I'd finally gotten my first sack of the year.

We won our fifth game at Utah State and I had a couple of hurries, but no sacks. There was a part of me that had begun to doubt; I wondered if I should change my goal or stick with it and find a way to make it become reality. I chose to stick with my goal.

We played against Brian Urlacher's New Mexico Lobos. I picked up four sacks in this cold, wet game. It had all finally come together, and I was riding high. In our next game, against UNLV, I picked up two second-half sacks, which put me at seven for the year. Teams began double-teaming me, which kept me without a sack until our bowl game against Marshall University, in which I sacked Chad Pennington three times. We lost that game in horrible fashion, but by the end of my junior year, I had reached my goal of ten sacks.

The big lesson? Don't lower your goals. Adjust your mentality and work ethic, and multiply your action ten times if necessary. Visualization is crucial to prosperity. If you see it with your mind's eye before it happens, you can create it in the external world. You create it spiritually and mentally before you create it physically.

I had momentum on my side heading into my senior year of college and football. In spite of my many injuries and trials, I had won. I kept winning because I kept getting back up after I got knocked down. But you know as well as I do that winning is a present-day occurrence. It's not about resting on past laurels and successes.

Questions to Consider Carefully and Answer:

- When you face adversity, what questions can you ask that will serve you powerfully and enable you to get what you want?
- How else can you view adversity instead of seeing it as something bad?
- Do you visualize success and happiness on a daily basis?
- What would happen if you began to visualize success in your job?
- Do you change your goals when the going gets hard, or do you increase your effort and shift strategy to hit your goals?

- What story are you telling yourself today? Does that story serve you or limit you?
- Do you *really* want what you say you want, or do you want it only if it comes easily?

CHAPTER 5

The Seeds of Greatness Arise through Adversity
Embrace It and Love It

| ı ı ı ı ı | ı ı ı ı ı | ı ı ı ı ı | ı ı ı ı ı | ı ı ı ı ı | ı ı ı ı ı | ı ı ı ı |

"Adversity is like a strong wind. It tears away
from us all but the things that cannot be torn,
so that we see ourselves as we really are."
—Arthur Golden

When I began my senior year at BYU, it was difficult to prepare for the season and what was to come. I couldn't play spring ball the semester before, and doubts filled my mind like a torrential downpour. I wasn't even sure I was going to be a starter that fall. But sitting out wasn't an option. I had been voted a team captain by my teammates, so I had to lead.

I had a few months to get my body ready after the shoulder surgery. Once again, my preparation preceded my power and confidence and I came into fall camp at 265 pounds. My body was strong, and my mind was ready to make a run for another double-digit sack season. My core was strong and solid, and my legs were fresh and ready to go. I felt great. I believed we had a chance to do something special that year.

We played Florida State in the first game. Brett Keisel had come back from Snow College, and between me, Ryan Denney, and Brett, we had a three-man wrecking crew on the ends, alongside returning starters Chris Hoke and Hans Olsen, who were both mammoths in the middle.

The problem was that we weren't nearly ready to be the team we wanted to be. We didn't have the key players we needed in the secondary. We dropped the season opener in the Pigskin Classic to Bobby Bowden's Florida State, 21–3. Our guys made mental mistakes, and our offense couldn't generate what we needed.

In the second game of the season, we made the long trip to the East Coast again and played Virginia. We were down 21–0 at the half. I knew we couldn't drop this game. As a captain, I talked with Kalani Sitake (who is now the head coach at BYU), and our other two captains, Margin Hooks and Jared Lee, about what adjustments we needed to make. We talked with the team before the coaches came in, and we made a plan to take it one play at a time and stay focused. We came out in the second half and made a furious run to tie the game, finishing regulation 35–35. We went on to win the game with a field goal in overtime.

In the third game of my senior year, we lost at Air Force. I picked up two sacks and once again had a great showing. Four sacks in three games had me feeling great. But I was unhappy with our team showing. How in the world were we 1–2 in my senior year?

In our first home game, Mississippi State spanked us on national television in a Thursday-night game aired on ESPN. We were 1–3 now and nowhere near where I'd thought we would be at this point in the year. I honestly thought we would be undefeated. That's how optimistic I was about our team and my play.

In the Mississippi State game, I rushed around the offensive tackle, a guy they'd nicknamed "Pork Chop." Thinking I had a sack, I dove for their quarterback. He felt the pressure and I fell on my shoulder. I got up and knew something was wrong. I couldn't feel my arm, and I had a sharp pain running down my arm and into my neck. The pain was intense, and I knew I'd hurt myself badly. In fact, I had separated my shoulder. Pain continued shooting up and down my arm, unlike anything I had ever felt before.

I had been prepared and ready to go, and now I was injured again. I cried silently to the heavens, *God, what's going on here? I've done everything you've asked me to do. I've prepped myself physically and mentally. Why is this happening to me? Why am I experiencing this?*

Of course, asking *why me* never works.

I struggled physically for the rest of that season. Our team also struggled. I ate humble pie throughout my senior year at BYU. I was taking cortisone shots for my shoulder, and getting weaker because I couldn't lift or practice hard. But I kept my rose-colored glasses on and stayed as positive as I could.

Finally, we were at 4–6, with two games to go in the season. Everyone wondered if this would be the season that Coach Edwards finished with a losing record. At the beginning of the season, he had announced that this would be his final dance. So in the final game at BYU stadium, Gordon B. Hinckley, president of the Church of Jesus Christ of Latter-day Saints, presided over a ceremony in which the arena was renamed "LaVell Edwards Stadium."

Despite my injuries, I had racked up eight sacks during the season. I was going to use the last two games to finish the job. During my final game at LaVell Edwards Stadium, I knocked the quarterback to the ground and my momentum carried me forward. My elbow hit the ground and I felt my shoulder pop out. I'd already separated the same shoulder in the Mississippi State game, and now I had dislocated it. I couldn't move it. I ran off the field and the doctor slipped it back into place. I ran back in and picked up my ninth sack of the season as I raced around the tackle without him so much as touching me.

In the third quarter, I came out of a two-point stance and strip-sacked the quarterback while Hans Olsen recovered the ball. Those two sacks got me to my goal of ten sacks for the season. I became the Mountain West Conference sack leader that year. I recorded ten sacks in my junior year and ten sacks in my senior year, for a total of twenty sacks in two seasons. Not bad for a guy who was sharing time with two other studs who would both go on to have awesome careers in the NFL. Again, I wasn't the strongest or the fastest of the group, but I always worked to keep that mental edge and found ways to maximize my production.

The final game of my college career arrived. We were playing the "Holy War" game against our rival, the University of Utah. I was beat up from fractures, concussions, back problems, shoulder injuries, and surgeries. There were moments in the season when my back was in so much pain I could barely stand up straight. For my final game of the season, against Utah, I wasn't much better off. I couldn't sleep the night before and I puked three times the day of the game. In the locker room, pre-game, I fell asleep on the floor for an hour—a nice "power nap."

The "Holy War" game became an instant classic. Their defense picked off the first pass of the game and took it to the house for a touchdown. Not exactly the start a team wants to see, but our offense was resilient. We battled and took a comfortable lead heading into the fourth quarter, with the score at 26–10.

Rivalry games are a different beast in which anything can happen—and it did. Utah scored seventeen straight points on us in the fourth quarter and the score was 27–26. I couldn't believe it. With 1:04 remaining on the clock and our offense backed up 4th and 13 deep in our own territory, it looked like Coach Edwards would indeed finish up with a losing season.

Then, with the clock ticking down the final minute of the game, our quarterback, Brandon Doman, threw a last-effort pass to the middle of the field. Mind you, Doman was our third-string quarterback, and he was filling in because our previous two quarterbacks were out. His pass hit the mark, though; it was caught by Jonathan Pittman, who made an adjustment on it and came back to catch it.

Nobody could believe it except us. Utah's pass defense was number one in the country that year. Then, on the very next play, Doman threw another deep pass down to the goal line, which was caught again by Pittman. A couple of plays later, Doman ran it in behind Kalani Sitake, Luke Staley, Tevita Ofahengaue, and our offensive line to take the lead. Our defense made the necessary stop against Utah's offense and we went on to win the game. LaVell Edwards had his miracle win at Utah to finish his career as a coaching legend.

The season couldn't have ended better. It had been a mediocre, injury-riddled season for my team and me. But we beat Utah that year and that capped off a tough season with some sweetness.

My senior year had been nothing like I'd thought it would be when we started the season. I'd envisioned a winning season, a national championship game, and an All-American campaign as the NCAA sack leader. The season had been anything but that. It was like a nightmare from which I couldn't wake up. Despite the anguish of losing so many games, fighting through injury, and doubting myself, I continued to pick myself up and move forward. I continued to lean on God and trust Him.

Facing the Fire
We all experience some type of adversity that tests our souls. We endure sickness, the death of loved ones, financial turmoil, bitter divorce, or other tragedies. If you're not ready to handle the hardship, then you can't earn the prizes in life that come to those willing not

only to endure suffering, but also to endure it well. You'll never get where you want to be in life unless you stay the course in the face of hardship. Remain committed to what you desire for your life, your family, and your business, no matter how big the vision and no matter how difficult the journey. If you're willing to go through the refiner's fire, you can reach your highest aspirations. You can turn your visions for your life into reality.

It was brutal to go through five shoulder surgeries, multiple concussions, a leg fracture, and back injuries during a time I had so eagerly anticipated. The injuries were a frustrating impediment to my determination to conquer. But injuries, whether I liked it or not, are part of the game of football.

In life, you will have other kinds of injuries. That's part of our experience on this ball of clay we call "Earth." You can blame, complain, and make excuses, or you can own your life and choose to be powerful regardless of external circumstances.

You can play the victim card or you can choose the "I am responsible" card. Are you willing to do whatever is necessary for you to grow and become the greatest version of yourself? Are you willing to face adversity to get to your promised land?

Making and losing money is part of the game of business. It happens even to the best of us. Broken hearts are part of the game of relationships and love. Sure, you can avoid heartache, but you'll miss out on the joy of being in deep, meaningful relationships that would help you grow and become the greatest version of yourself.

Fear, doubt, and pain—they are all part of the game of life. How beautiful and divine are the gifts of fear and doubt. Fear allows us to exercise courage. Doubt allows us to choose faith.

When adversity hits, you decide what you're going to do with it. It's not easy. But it doesn't have to be hard. The adversity I went through forged a power inside me that can't be bought or taught, and can't be taken away. You can't go through adversity and not be affected somehow, but how you deal with adversity will determine how you see life. Is it a world of opportunity? Or a dead end? The choice is yours.

Questions to Consider Carefully and Answer:

- What needs to shift inside you to enable you to view life's natural obstacles in a way that would serve and empower you?
- What would your life look like if you chose to embrace those difficulties to learn lessons rather than getting angry and shutting down?
- What opportunities have come into your life because of things you wouldn't have chosen?
- What lessons can you learn right now from your current afflictions and difficulties?

CHAPTER 6

The Truth about Gifts
"Seek Ye the Best Gifts"

|₁₁₁₁₁|₁₁₁₁₁|₁₁₁₁₁|₁₁₁₁₁|₁₁₁₁₁|₁₁₁₁₁|₁₁₁₁

*"It is your responsibility to use your talents wisely
and it is your right to enjoy the process."*
—**Allison Rimm**, *The Joy of Strategy*

Whether you believe it or not, you have gifts and talents that are unique to you. The whole purpose of our unique abilities and gifts is to create value for other people. Life becomes enjoyable and genuinely meaningful when you find, develop, and utilize those gifts and talents to serve others. I call this "creating value."

During my time at BYU, when I wasn't playing football, I spoke and presented to church groups, school groups, and everything in between. I spoke to children, young men and women, adults, scout groups, and any other groups that wanted me to come and speak. As an ambassador for BYU and the football program, I had countless opportunities to share messages of positivity, hope, and encouragement. Because of my success as a student athlete, I had more opportunity to influence others and create value for them.

I love speaking. I learned early on that making a difference for other people through the power of the spoken word makes me feel really good about myself and about others. I feel it is part of my life's calling. As a child, I believed in my heart—just as I believe now—that speaking and training are my gifts. I realized that if I chose to develop those gifts, God would help me to help others on Earth. I also discovered that the bigger the stage, the more I loved it. The more there was on the line, the more I thrived.

Certain conditions bring about certain results. Fertile soil allows seeds to sprout. Great nutrition and fitness produces a physique that allows greater performance.

What allows our gifts to reveal themselves so we can better use them? The answer is *adversity*. Adversity exposes weakness and forces us to dig deep into our souls to grow and become more powerful. I found in myself gifts and talents I wouldn't have seen without the hardships I endured, and those hardships inspired in me the desire to do great things. And I was about to get a heavy dose of adversity in my days after BYU.

Once my senior season finished, it was time to find an agent to represent me for the NFL. I interviewed four agents to see who could best help me as I prepared for that next step. I hadn't decided on one yet when Shirley, our guardian angel of the football office, told me that one more agent wanted to talk to me. Suddenly I had that familiar feeling, that sensation of a voice telling me that I should give this agent a chance.

Steve Dubin walked into my home and I knew right away that he was the real deal. He might as well have walked in with custom clothing that read *LEGIT*, because that's how I felt when he began to talk. His demeanor was professional and commanding. Dubin and his partner,

Don Yee, represented Tom Brady, Frank Wycheck, Steve Mariucci, and a number of other great professional players and coaches. Steve told me he wasn't interested in players who didn't have great character or who needed babysitting. He knew I could be a brilliant pass-rush specialist off the line on third downs in the NFL. I was the caliber of player they wanted for their firm.

It's gratifying to have someone tell you they believe in you. Between my surgeries and my inability to perform at the NFL Combine, I was already beginning to doubt myself. I remember how I felt when Steve articulated his and Don's confidence in me: In that moment, I vowed one day to be in a position to speak powerfully to others who might have have forgotten their own power.

Gifts from Adversity

After I signed with Yee and Dubin, they stayed in touch while I rehabbed my shoulder.

After a few months, Don Yee asked me point-blank, "Do you want to play this game?"

My obvious answer was a resounding "Yes!"

He replied, "We need you to get ready. When you're recovered from your injury, we'll get you workouts for teams. But it'll be up to you to make it."

I knew without a doubt I would make a team; I just needed the opportunity. An opportunity with the Chargers soon presented itself. They signed me, but when they learned the extent of my injury, they sent me back home. Once again, another wall had sprung up before me.

During that spring and summer of 2001, three very powerful things came about because of my injury and time away from football. What I'd initially viewed only as adversity turned out to be an opportunity to achieve things I'd never even imagined. Sometimes hindsight is the only way we recognize blessings, so it's critical to keep moving forward no matter how difficult things may seem.

The summer of 2001 stretched before me. I had no schoolwork because I had graduated. I couldn't work out because of my shoulder. What was I supposed to do now?

I'd always wanted to learn to play the piano, but I didn't know how to read music. I could play basic chords on the guitar, and I could sing, but the most I could play on piano was "Chopsticks" and a couple of basic chords. But it so happened that a beautiful girl I knew also played piano, and she volunteered to teach me.

When she taught me the very first song I'd ever learned, something came over me and the notes began flowing easily. I started sitting at the piano every day and practicing over and over and over. It was pure memorization. I didn't acknowledge it at the time, but the opportunity to play the piano had only arisen due to the unfortunate condition of my shoulder. Adversity, as it happened, had turned into opportunity.

My world had opened up because I had time; I had nothing going on except rehab and piano. For the next couple of months, I dedicated my time to playing the piano. I sometimes played three to four hours a day, practicing songs over and over, sometimes until midnight. I'm sure my parents were thinking, *Please, NFL, take our son out of our home!* Learning a musical instrument is fun for the person who's learning, but not fun for everyone else who hears the same song a thousand-plus times, mistakes and all. But when you learn a skill—be it an instrument or a sport—and you're good at it, it becomes fun.

So the first blessing in disguise that came from my injuries was the gift of music. The neat thing about being able to play the piano was that I could reach people I couldn't have reached otherwise. I played in spiritual firesides that permitted me to continue making a difference in the lives of others and helping them to feel the abundant love of God through music.

As a result of learning the piano, I gained the opportunity to play in a band called Mana Poly All-Stars from 2003 to 2010, following my days in the NFL. We dropped two albums in that time, and we traveled and played all over. I have great memories of experiences I shared with my brothers and sister from that band.

I also played for an island performance group called Taimane. We performed at luaus all over the state of Utah. What a blessing music has been for me!

The second gift that came to me during this time was getting to know my best friend, Laina, the gal who'd taught me that first song on the piano. As we spent more time together, I began to love her as much more than just a friend.

Laina and I spent the majority of our time together in the summer of 2001. She helped me to stay as active as possible with my shoulder rehab: We worked out, played ball, and ran. If we weren't working out or playing ball, we'd sit at my home and sing along to the few songs I could play on the piano. Sometimes we'd just hang out, talk on the phone, or go out to grab food during what we called "midnight runs." She became my best friend.

The third gift that came as a result of my injuries was delivered when I was finally ready to play football again. It was a gift that would take me to the Super Bowl. It began when my agent finally told me, "OK, we have three teams you're going to be working out for: New England, San Francisco, and Philadelphia. It's up to you now."

Making the Right Decision

I flew to Boston to work out with the Patriots, and reality set in as soon as I got there. I was nervous. I ate more than five thousand calories a day to gain weight. At BYU I'd finished my senior year at just under 260 pounds. That off-season I ate like a horse and was relentless in the gym. Now I was 285 pounds and in great shape. My shoulder was strong.

I was bench-pressing, shoulder-pressing, jumping, running, and doing everything I needed to do to be able to succeed. Romeo Crennel, the defensive coordinator, worked me out. Pepper Johnson came out and helped out as well.

A week later, I flew to San Francisco and worked out with the 49ers. The following week, I flew back out to the East Coast to work out with the Philadelphia Eagles. By the time I got home from the Eagles trip, I felt discouraged. I thought, *What's the point?* My back was already giving me major trouble. I continued to pray to God, asking for guidance on what I should do with my life. But the moment I was ready to move on from football and hang up my cleats, I got a call from New England. They wanted to sign me immediately. I couldn't have been more excited. The next day, I got a call from the San Francisco 49ers.

They said, "We have an injured player and want to bring you out immediately."

The problem was that I had already given my word to New England that I was signing with them.

San Francisco said, "No big deal. It's business. We're on the West Coast and you're in Utah. You'll have a greater opportunity here because of the scheme we run."

Something inside me kept saying, *No, you are not supposed to go to San Francisco.* But I *wanted* to go to the 49ers. It seemed like a no-brainer. San Francisco had been my team growing up because of '80s and '90s superstars like Steve Young, Joe Montana, and Ronnie Lott. Plus, it was on the West Coast. But the voice inside me kept saying, *No. You said you're going to New England and that's where you've got to go.* So I signed with the New England Patriots.

That decision led me to a Super Bowl championship team and forever changed my life. I heeded that familiar feeling inside, one that I've felt often throughout my life, and it grew into amazing things, just as the adversity I'd faced had led me down the path to growth.

Adversity had given me opportunities to grow, and although there were dark times between my senior year and the day when I finally got into the NFL, I'd remained optimistic, dedicated, and committed. The game of college was done. I loved this woman who was now my best friend. I'd learned to play the piano. And I'd signed with the Patriots. I'd won. Next up? The NFL.

No matter how difficult your life is right now, there are gifts available to you if you're open to receiving them. Some things you will only be able to see in hindsight. My gifts didn't materialize until I'd stepped through the darkness. Keep moving your life forward. You were born with a higher purpose and plan. It's up to you to discover it, create it, and **choose it**.

Questions to Consider Carefully and Answer:

- What gifts do you have that allow you to live a fulfilled life, serve others, and create joy in your heart?
- What unique abilities have you developed as a result of adversity and affliction?
- What are your natural talents and abilities that, if developed, could become a great vehicle to make a difference in the lives of others?
- Are you seeking to know and live your gifts and talents?
- What holds you back from listening to that voice within?

CHAPTER 7

Iron Sharpens Iron
The Catalyst of Brotherhood

| ι ι ι ι ι | ι ι ι ι ι | ι ι ι ι ι | ι ι ι ι ι | ι ι ι ι ι | ι ι ι ι ι | ι ι ι ι

"Iron sharpeneth iron; so a man sharpeneth the countenance of his friend."
—Proverbs 27:17

The Rams tied the game in the fourth quarter, leaving very little time to do anything on offense. Should we kneel on the ball and force overtime, or try to win Super Bowl XXXVI in regulation?

"Let's go!" was the message from the coaches as we prepared to make an assault on the Rams' defense with 1:30 remaining in regulation. Brady hit some short passes and we kept chipping away at the defense.

As I watched from the sideline, my heart raced and adrenaline filled my body. I knew we had something special going on. After all, the last team we'd lost to during the regular season had been the Rams, also known as "The Greatest Show on Turf." But this time, it seemed like everything was lining up for us to win.

Every day we had practiced "situational" football by simulating a two-minute drill as if it were the end of the game and we were losing. We practiced running the field-goal unit out and kicking the field goal. So everyone knew how much time we needed on the clock to properly execute this. Everyone on the team was mentally and physically prepared to do what was required to win in any given situation.

Adam Vinatieri walked onto the field with seven seconds remaining in regulation and kicked the ball perfectly, right through the goal posts. And just like that, the Super Bowl was over. We had won the game and were now world champions.

No words could adequately express the feelings you have when you win a game of such magnitude. Quite simply, it's unbelievable. You work so many hours, days, weeks, months, and years to have this chance. When you come out victorious, there is nothing in this world like it.

BELIEVE

After the Chargers signed me in 2001 and then sent me home because of my shoulder injury and surgery, I continued to believe I would make it. I followed up that belief with ruthless work. While all my college teammates were already playing on NFL teams, I was still nursing and rehabbing my shoulder.

Before I arrived in New England, I knew I just needed to catch a break. I believed in myself and kept mentally saying, *Give me a shot, and I'll make it.* I believed in myself long before my efforts bore fruit, and you must do the same.

Can you believe in yourself when no one else does?

Can you choose to believe that good things will come no matter how difficult your past is?

Can you believe in the good in people, regardless of how badly you've been treated?

Can you believe in something you can't see, operating out of faith and trusting that it can happen?

DO YOUR JOB
When I first got to New England, there was a phrase Bill Belichick used all the time: "Do your job."

He said this thirty to forty times a day. I understand why guys love Belichick so much: Bill loves his job, his coaching staff, and his players. He preaches the "Do Your Job" mentality, and lives he it. He is the epitome of the mantra *"DO YOUR JOB."*

My job as a defensive end was to not worry about the corner or the safety or even the linebacker. My job is my job, and if I focus on that, I have faith that my team will handle their business. They have faith in me to do my job, and I have faith in them to do theirs.

People who do not attain success focus on everything but the necessary required actions. Their minds drift easily, and they get pulled in every direction by social media, e-mail, gossip, the news, and other things outside their control. People who generally avoid their jobs tend to live out their lives lacking happiness and success. It's easier to pretend to be doing a job than to actually do it.

People who do attain success in life focus on the necessary required information, steps, and actions. **In short, they focus on their jobs, period.**

What is your job as a parent, spouse, salesman, marketer, manager, or CEO? What's your responsibility? What's your stewardship? On a plane, before a flight, you are told to put your mask on first before helping someone else put his/her mask on. Do your job first and then support others in helping them to do their jobs. A fast path to misery is to try to perform someone else's job for them when he is more than capable of doing it for himself. Another path to misery is to get caught up in other people's business when we are best served by focusing on our own business.

How do you win games? *By doing your job.*

How do you level up your marriage? *By doing your job.*

How do you create powerful relationships with your children? *By doing your job.*

How can you ensure that you succeed in sports and in work? *By doing your job.*

Doing your job requires total responsibility and accountability. Doing your job also requires that you *know* your job. It's almost impossible to do your job well if you are ignorant or incompetent.

Get the Edge

During fall camp in 2002, I came into the locker room and announced, "Man, I just ate some McDonald's."

The place went quiet. Richard Seymour, the first-round draft pick of the year before, said, "Come here, man."

We sat down and he asked a bunch of the guys around us what they'd had for lunch. Some guys had eaten chicken and rice, or fish and broccoli with lemon water. I'd eaten a Double Quarter Pounder with Cheese and had extra fries. I realized that I still didn't understand what it meant to be a professional.

Seymour said, "You've got to understand; this is our game. You're looking for every possible edge. If the guy you're competing against is equal to you, what will give you the edge? You have to learn to use your nutrition and anything else you can to help yourself."

I never forgot that lesson. If you and the people you're competing with are equal and have everything in common, you have to find an edge—a way to gain an advantage. Sometimes it may just be the food you eat. If you truly want to be a professional, you're going to have to learn to find the edge. You're going to have to learn to find it in your marriage, your relationships, and your sales negotiations. Your edge may be in your listening skills, your work ethic, or something else that will help you become the greatest version of yourself.

Be Your Word

Another lesson I learned was from Willie McGinest, a first-round draft pick out of USC in 1994. He's a phenomenal player with a big heart, and I'll never forget when he asked me if I wanted to go out to eat with him and some of the other players after practice.

I replied, "Yeah, sure, I'll be there."

He looked at me and asked, "Hey, man, are you just saying that, and you're not really going to show up, like a lot of Polynesians back home?" He was right on the money.

The truth was, I wasn't planning to show up, and he called me out on it. It was crazy, because I couldn't believe that he knew I was just saying it and didn't mean it. I knew that wasn't how I wanted to be remembered. I knew that my word had to matter. I decided right then that from that day forward, if I say I'm going to be somewhere, I've got to *be there*—or simply say no to the request.

Actualizing your word is powerful. I've learned in the NFL and in business that to be trusted and relied upon is one of the greatest strengths a man or woman can have. There is a power that we develop inside ourselves the moment we begin to honor our word and speak from that place of power and certainty. If you want your confidence to skyrocket, the fastest and surest way to see that happen is to make and keep commitments. Just keep your word. It really works ... and when you don't honor your word, nothing works.

The Tuck Rule in the Snow

One of the highlights of that winning season was a divisional play-off game that meant the difference between moving on to the Super Bowl or going home. We drove the ball down the field in a back-and-forth game. Snow was falling hard, and during halftime, quarters, and time-outs, the snowblowers came out to clear the yard lines. We needed three points to tie the game, or a touchdown to take the lead against the Raiders.

Tom Brady dropped back to pass on that critical drive to stay in the game, and he got hit and fumbled the ball. The game was over. I couldn't believe it. I was furious that we were now out of the play-off race after a magical season. The Raiders sideline celebrated, with their sights now set on Pittsburgh for the AFC championship game. Our season was over.

Then something stunning happened. The referees gathered and began discussing the fumble. I couldn't believe it; it was crazy. We got the ball back and somehow we were back in it. Vinatieri came out and kicked a long field goal in the snow to send the game into overtime. We won the game in overtime and found ourselves headed to the AFC championship game against the Steelers.

The lesson here is that when you're ready to give up, when the game seems like it's over, you've got to keep fighting. Even if you're losing, keep fighting. There's no guarantee that you'll win if you continue to fight, but if you give up and *don't* fight, it's *guaranteed* that you'll lose. The football gods wore Patriots gear that day.

When I first arrived in New England, I was nervous and homesick. My only solace was my teammates, who welcomed me. My locker was next to the locker of fellow rookie Matt Light, who was as positive and upbeat as anyone I'd ever met. Ty Law was one of the first guys to come up and introduce himself to me. After I'd met the other players—Joe Andruzzi, Tom Brady, Drew Bledsoe, Troy Brown, and David Patten, among others—I wondered, *Can I even play at this level?*

I had my doubts, which is normal. If you're working on improving yourself or your life, you're going to face challenges that bring doubt into your mind all the time. Ignore the doubts. Exercise faith. Choose to believe and focus on doing your job. One of my favorite quotes is "Doubt your doubts before you doubt your faith."

When you start anything new, you're going to have an abundance of doubt. When you begin a business, a relationship, or anything difficult and potentially life changing, doubt will show up like a shotgun in your face, a ninja who can't be seen but is nonetheless lethal. That's part of any new phase of anyone's life. Instead of choosing to give energy and attention to doubt, choose faith and hard work. That's what I focused on. After beating the Raiders in that play-off game, we went to Pittsburgh. I knew we were going to win the AFC championship game. It was a close game, and Brady got injured, so Drew Bledsoe came in to lead us to the Super Bowl.

We flew to New Orleans the day after we beat Pittsburgh. This was one of my greatest dreams coming true. I couldn't believe we were at the Super Bowl. It was unreal. One year earlier, I had been a college senior struggling with all these injuries. Now I was playing with the New England Patriots at the Super Bowl. So many men work hard and never make it there. I felt that God had allowed this to be a part of my life, and I expressed daily gratitude and deep appreciation for the opportunity. I'd never won a state championship, although I'd always had my sights set on one, and I hadn't won an outright conference championship in college. But the Super Bowl would more than suffice.

At times I still couldn't believe we were there. Hanging out with celebrities as a rookie right out of college was fascinating to me. All of us players had our cameras out like we were little kids. My heart continued to swell with gratitude. As a member of the Church of Jesus Christ of Latter-day Saints, I live by a strict health code that requires me to avoid tobacco, alcohol, and coffee. My teammates were very protective of my beliefs, and when we went out, they'd say things like, "Hey, we're watching man," or "This guy will take a Sprite; he's Mormon." It wasn't at all how Hollywood portrays it. It couldn't have been more ideal.

When we won the Super Bowl, we ran onto the field. It was truly one of the greatest moments I've ever experienced in my life. It was a dream come true. We'd prepared as a team, and we'd walked out as a team, which is now how it's done in the Super Bowl.

Unable to Stand Up and Walk

Six months later in fall camp, I couldn't stand up straight. The truth is, I had been in pain for a few years, but so much focus had been placed on my shoulder that I'd just ignored my back. It was so painful that the injections did nothing at all for me. It got to the point where I couldn't take it any longer and took a couple of days off. I was told that if I wanted to play, I could have surgery. But surgery wasn't part of my plan and I knew it.

I prayed, *God, if this isn't right, just let me know, and I'll be done with football.* I asked the Lord to help me with this decision. Looking back on my life, I saw myself as a young boy with a red notebook and dreams. Then I saw myself as a player constantly riddled with back pain. My back had bothered me in high school and at BYU. It had bothered me in the mission field. It was a truth I could no longer ignore. I knew in my heart it was time to move on.

When it's time to move on, you do it, whether it's a job, a relationship, or football. If you know you've given 100 percent, and the voice within is saying, *You're done,* then there's no regret in moving on. You have to know you left everything on the field, and leave with no doubts.

In the spring of 2003, I officially retired. I was done playing ball. I'd had a very short career, not really long enough to even call it a career. But it was a privilege to have been a part of the New England Patriots. In the time I was there, I learned great lessons from great men. I'm grateful to the older players, the vets, who took time to teach me—like Anthony Pleasant, who passed out literature about how to take care of family. I'm also grateful to the players with whom I had Bible study during the week. It was a great group of guys who were trying to keep a job, trying to make it in life, and trying to stay there.

The downside to being so focused on making the team and competing was that I had missed out on some crucial lessons. I wasn't very good at taking care of my money; I had made a decent amount of it, but I wasn't smart with it. I just spent it as if it were going to keep coming in. People think, *All these guys in the NFL are making a lot of money,* but the fact is, they're generally not making all *that* much. Even if a guy is making $500,000 a year, he's going to give half of it to taxes. Then he has to travel back and forth from home to where he works and try to keep up some type of lifestyle. It's tough. If I could go back and do it again, I wouldn't have spent the money like I did. Hindsight is always twenty-twenty.

They don't teach money smarts in college. They don't teach you how to manage and save money. Or maybe they do; I just didn't sign up for that class.

When you make money, you think, *This is going to be great! Let me spend it; let me buy some stuff, fly first class, get massages, hire trainers, and buy new clothes and new shoes.* Then you have family and friends asking you for money and it can be difficult to say no. In my second season, I overheard many of the veterans telling the rookies NOT to buy the cars, and NOT to spend the money. But most of the rookies showed up in brand-new cars anyway.

Sometimes the only way to learn is the hard way, and that's all right as long as you do learn. When you start making money, start saving. Put it away. Learn to live on less than you earn, because if you don't, you'll find yourself in trouble. This was a lesson I would learn the hard way—not once, but twice.

You probably have something in your life that means as much to you as the NFL meant to me. It's a dream and a possibility. Making the NFL or winning a Super Bowl ring feels great only if you've done the work to get there. There's no satisfaction in being handed something you didn't earn. People in positions of power love to earn what they receive, and work for the prizes and promised lands. I am forever grateful for the time I had as a professional athlete in the NFL. Even though the time was short and my back still gives me major fits, I wouldn't do it any other way.

Questions to Consider Carefully and Answer:

- Why would it be important to create empowering beliefs inside you that supports your making it to *your* "NFL"?
- Do you know what your "job" is, and are you doing it daily? If yes, what can you do better? If no, what's getting in the way and what can you do to overcome that?
- What's *one thing* you can do today to find that edge in your workplace, your marriage, your family, and your spirituality?
- Can people count on you and trust you? Are you your word, or do you find yourself making up excuses and stories to explain to people why you don't fulfill your promises?
- Do you believe life has more to offer you? If so, what are you doing about it? If not, what can you do to change that perspective?

CHAPTER 8

Starting Over, but Not Really
Using the Past to Propel the Future

| ı ı ı ı ı | ı ı ı ı ı | ı ı ı ı ı | ı ı ı ı ı | ı ı ı ı ı | ı ı ı ı ı | ı ı ı ı ı |

"Change is inevitable. Progress is optional."
—Tony Robbins

W hen I came home from the NFL, I was confused and depressed. Uncertainty about my future loomed over me. Football had been a huge part of my life for so long, and now it was over. I couldn't believe it. I had worked out and practiced for thousands of hours. I'd gone from playing at LaVell Edwards stadium in Provo, Utah to playing in huge stadiums across the country to being part of a Super Bowl championship. Through it all, I easily put in ten thousand to twenty thousand hours of football, mentally and physically. Now I was done.

For the first week, I lay in bed in my mom's basement. I watched TV and ate ice cream that entire week. I was depressed and cried like a baby. This made me feel embarrassed and ashamed. But I finally came to accept the fact that football was done; it was time to move on.

After a week, I got my bearings and thought, *OK, it's time to go. What's next?* I tried a telemarketing job, which involved doing sales in a warehouse. I was setting guys up to close deals for personal coaching. After a few weeks of this nonsense, I realized I hated it. *This is horrible,* I thought. *This is not my purpose. This isn't what I'm supposed to do. I was meant for more. I was built for more. I played professional football and won a Super Bowl. I received a college degree from a great university. I've always been a leader. Why am I doing this sleazy job?*

I'm not saying that salespeople are sleazy; I love sales. But this company was crooked. We were charging people $10,000 to $15,000 to be coached by some guy who read from a book while the "coach" made $20 an hour. Are you kidding me? That's not real coaching. That's dishonest. I wouldn't have sold that to my parents, and I didn't feel good about it. So I moved on to the next thing.

I looked at different jobs and opportunities and I thought I had more value than I really did, but no one told me otherwise. I was confident in my work ethic, and I knew I could succeed in whatever I did.

One of my close friends was selling mortgages. When he told me how much money he was making, I couldn't believe it. Then he showed me his check, and I saw that he drove a brand-new car; that's when I decided to get into the mortgage business.

I started selling mortgages in 2003, and that first year was pathetic. I'd show up at the office in my slippers around noon. I think I made $25,000 that year, which is not very impressive at all. Most of the folks in the office told me later that they didn't think I'd make it. It's a wonder that I did.

There is a high cost for not treating your job like a profession. If you treat it like a hobby, as I did, you'll get paid like you would for a hobby. If you decide to become a professional, however, you can get paid like a professional. In football, I was a professional. But in my early days of selling mortgages, I was an amateur.

Here are some distinctions between professional and amateur. See what applies to you:

Amateurs practice till they get it right.
Professionals practice till they can't do it wrong.

Amateurs operate on *shoulds*.
Professionals operate on *musts*.

Amateurs act only when they feel like it and let circumstances dictate what they do.
Professionals act decisively in spite of feelings and moods.

Amateurs mismanage expectations.
Professionals create agreements and abide by them.

Amateurs hope and wish for success.
Professionals do what's required to succeed.

Amateurs think you have to be in the right place at the right time to succeed.
Professionals know that the right time is now and the right place is here.

Amateurs want everything for free.
Professionals aren't afraid to pay the price for what they want.

Amateurs always have reasons and excuses.
Professionals create results.

Amateurs say "maybe" and "let me think on that."
Professionals operate in "yes" and "no."

Amateurs quit if they don't get immediate results.
Professionals stay committed to getting results, regardless of how long it takes.

Amateurs explain things away with long stories.
Professionals speak succinctly and powerfully.

Which are you right now? Are you still an amateur, or have you turned pro yet? In January 2004, I made up my mind to become a professional and decided to apply to the mortgage industry the same focus and effort I'd devoted to football. I knew without a doubt that if I approached mortgages like I'd approached football, I would succeed. I couldn't keep living like I had been living. I refused to believe that my best days were behind me, although I was tempted to settle and just accept the status quo. You, too, will be tempted to think that your best days are behind you, especially if you've accomplished some great things early in your life. Don't believe it. Your best days are right in front of you if you'll live that way.

Learners Are Earners

I set a goal in January of 2004 to make six figures for the year. Several people told me it was an unrealistic goal because I was so new in the industry and they had only seen the uncommitted, amateur Setema the year before. What they didn't know is that when I get serious and committed, I go all out, like I did in getting the sacks in football. It was a MUST for me that year. I knew I had a moral obligation to continue to expand, grow, and become all God had created me to be. I'm grateful that the broker with whom I was working that year decided to take a chance on me and give me an office. I'm sure he didn't think I'd make it either.

I hired my first consultant and was terrified by the cost. He charged me $500 a month—a lot of money to me back then—but he promised me that he could help me generate business with his system. Within the first two months of hiring this consultant, I made more than enough to pay him for twelve months. That was my first lesson in hiring real consultants. **When you hire the right people, and do the required work, you get incredible results.** The second lesson was this: **When you invest in yourself and do the work, the returns always come.**

In addition to setting this big goal for myself that year, I also bought a new truck and named it "Money." It was a green Chevy Avalanche. At the time, my car was dying and I thought, *If I buy this truck then I have to produce.* It was definitely a risk for me, but I needed a car and something to motivate me.

I hustled like crazy. I didn't know anything about mortgages, marketing, clients, or customer service. After all, football had been my main focus for many years. It seemed everyone was refinancing, and there were a lot of mortgage programs available. It was also easy to buy a home, and it seemed a lot of people were buying. I was relentless in what I did; I interviewed the best in my office, and the older folks were very helpful. And then I did what they told me to do and it worked.

I surpassed my goal that year by 50 percent. I was single, twenty-eight years old, and had a bank account filled with money. The next problem I faced was that I was scared. I wondered, *Can I do this again?*

I was fearful that I wouldn't be able to replicate what I'd done in 2004. For some reason, I had this notion that money and prosperity were simply products of luck. I needed to get out of the scarcity mind-set. Throughout this time, I constantly talked to my best friend, Laina, who would end up becoming my wife.

She told me, "Of course you'll do it again. You just did it."

Hearing her reassuring words was all I needed.

In 2005, I more than doubled what I'd made in 2004. In 2006, I nearly quadrupled what I'd made in 2005. Throughout the entire time I was selling mortgages—and later, conducting real estate and hard-money deals—I felt confused. There was this emptiness inside me that came upon me at least once a month. I loved creating value for people, and I loved having money in my bank account. I loved being able to shop and to pick up dinner tabs. It was amazing to have this independent life, and to own my time and money. I could do anything I wanted to do.

But I was empty. I couldn't figure it out. I knew there was something more for me to do in my life, but what was it?

Taking Risks in Business

I started working in real estate. I bought homes, fixed them up, and flipped them to make more money. I kept some houses and had tenants. Doing this, in conjunction with the mortgage business, I made more money than I'd ever thought was possible growing up. And yet, the empty feeling inside me persisted. I lacked purpose and fulfillment in my work.

Soon I began lending money to people, although I had no idea what I was doing. My trusting nature, while a virtue at times, became my Achilles' heel when the economy took a turn and I ran out of money. At one time, I had about half a million dollars of my own money out in loans. I would lend it and people would pay me back with interest—and I had some pretty steep interest rates. I also started getting into properties around the country, picking up properties in Florida, Utah, Nevada, and Georgia.

I was acting arrogantly and ignorantly. I thought this prosperity wave and increase in home values would continue. Little did I know that what was coming down the pipe would nearly destroy me.

The sad part is that an older friend of mine actually told me, "You'd better be careful." Even my parents told me, "Son, what's going on is not sustainable."

I didn't listen. I thought, *Of course it can sustain. Look at me. I'm the man. I'm just this guy who knows how to do it.* I had leveraged out the mortgage business, real estate business, and hard-money lending business. I had properties in multiple states. I really wasn't prepared for what was about to hit.

Amid all this, deep down in my heart, I knew there was something more for me to do. Stephen Covey had a phrase that he used that resonated deeply with me: "Unleash human potential." I wrote this phrase in my journal and knew my role on Earth was to unleash human potential. In 2006 I attended a one-day workshop. They asked questions like, "If money were no object, what would you do with your life?" "If you were financially free, what would you do?" "With whom would you spend your time?" They were questions similar to the ones I've asked you throughout this book. These questions opened up my eyes; I wanted to have a life of meaningful contribution, growth, service, and fulfillment.

There Are No Bad Jobs

Life is too short to do anything that's not in line with your purpose and desires. I truly believe that every human being can do something that he or she is passionate about and that can allow him or her to make money *and* make a real difference in the world. There are no bad jobs, just opportunities to learn lessons. I learned a lot from working in mortgages, real estate, hard-money loans, investments, and properties. But I was hollow inside and constantly looking for something else.

If you're honest, and you're searching, there's something out there that you were built to do. There's something that would really fill your cup until it overflows. There's something that you can do to make great money, make a real difference, and provide value to the marketplace—something that would enable you to love your life.

I admire two guys: Tony Robbins, and the late Stephen R. Covey, who wrote *The 7 Habits of Highly Effective People*. I read Covey's book in 1995 and it completely changed my life. I have looked up to Tony Robbins and listened to many of his programs. I've dreamed of being the guy on the stage, with the influence and ability to make a difference. That was—and still is—my real passion: teaching, speaking, coaching, and influencing.

You've got to have the courage to walk away from what you're doing in order to pursue your highest purpose, especially when you're experiencing real success in your current work. I had the courage to walk away. People thought I was crazy. I had this vision that I could make a difference like Covey, Robbins, and other speakers. I attended workshops and seminars, and I'd see people speaking and think, *I can do it just as well as he can*, or *I can be better than him*.

I obviously had a lot of ego, and the competitiveness of football had fed that ego. That's not necessarily a bad thing. You've really got to have this piece of you that says, *I can be the best*, or *I AM the best*. But you have to balance it with respect and humility as you learn and work your way up the ladder.

Inside you there's something calling you to rise up and change. It begs you to focus, follow through, and fulfill. Something inside you may be saying, *It's time*. Listen to that feeling. While many positive, warm-and-fuzzy speakers say, "It's not too late," I boldly declare that if you don't listen and take immediate action, it *will* be too late. And it would've quickly been too late for me if I hadn't listened. Fate would have forced me to make a drastic move.

Questions to Consider Carefully and Answer:

- If money weren't an object:
    - What would you spend your time doing?
    - With whom would you spend your time?
    - What would you do for work?
- What gives you fulfillment and satisfaction and allows you to make a great living doing it?
- Where can you contribute more than what you are currently giving to your work, your family, and your relationships?
- What would it take for you to walk away from your current daily activities and do something else if you knew there was something else for you to do?
- Why is investing in yourself so important and mission-critical for your life?
- Is there a song inside you waiting to be sung?

CHAPTER 9

God Sends an Angel
When a Man Loves a Woman

| | | | | | | | | | | | | | | | | | | | | | | | | | | | | | | | | | | | | | |

"It is not a lack of love, but a lack of friendship
that makes unhappy marriages."
—Friedrich Nietzsche

I t was a hot July day in 2005 and I was turning twenty-nine. For my twenty-ninth birthday, my best friend—Laina—threw a surprise party for me. My family and friends came out for the occasion. In Polynesian culture, particularly Samoan culture, there is always a lot of joking and clowning around. This party was no different; my friends and family members told story after embarrassing story. We laughed, talked, sang, ate, and had a great time. At the end of the night, I realized it was all because of Laina. Here, my family was united and making memories and at the center of it all was this wonderful woman.

My parents got divorced when I was in fourth grade, and it really shook me. It was emotionally traumatic, and as a result, I became afraid of commitment. I knew I didn't want to get divorced when I got married, and for a long time, that fear prevented me from getting into a serious relationship.

I'll be honest; I loved dating. I would date all kinds of girls. I didn't discriminate. It didn't matter what color their skin was, or if they were athletic, nonathletic, tall, short, musical, nonmusical. I wanted to date different girls so I could have an idea what kind of woman I would someday marry. I was determined that on the day I said "Yes," I would say it with 100 percent certainty. And no one made me feel the way Laina did. I had dated many women, but I'd always returned home, picked up the phone, and called Laina. We had a blast together, and we had something special. Other guys talked about how beautiful, spiritual, athletic, musical, and smart she was. She was *my* ideal woman, too; I just didn't realize it at first. Back in high school, I had described in my red journal the type of woman that I wanted in my life. The crazy thing is, I still didn't realize that this was her.

When I came home from the NFL, she lived in St. Louis, Missouri, which wasn't a problem because we had stayed close. I'd fly to St. Louis to visit her and she'd fly to Utah to visit me. Whenever I heard her name, chills ran up and down my body. Something—a spark, a fire—lit up inside me.

We went on a few dates before our friendship blossomed. I knew that dating was the sifting process, and I was willing to sift and sort till I found my wife. I only wanted to get married once, so I had to be absolutely sure.

On a warm August evening in 2000, I called her house.

She assumed I was calling for another girl and told me, "Oh, she's not here."

I calmly replied, "I'm not calling for her; I'm calling for you." I wanted her to tell me about my family in Missouri. She agreed and I was in; my skills had worked. I picked her up and we went to Jamba Juice. I pulled out every move I had while we sat there. I even got out my guitar and sang to her (you could say I was extremely confident).

When I told her I played football, she rolled her eyes and said, "Every guy plays football." She wasn't impressed at all.

When I dropped her off later that evening, I said, "Thanks for the date."

"This wasn't a date," she replied.

I told her, "I picked you up, opened the car door for you, paid for your drink, sang to you, and dropped you off. It was a date."

That date was the first of many that fall. Over the next twelve months, she became my best friend.

We spent the summer of 2001 together. She taught me piano and worked out with me, and gradually, a deep bond was forged. One thing I learned early on about relationships is that you can't force great chemistry. And I had chemistry with this girl.

I still dated as many girls as I could, but after every date, I'd come home at night and call Laina. I'd tell her about the girls I was hanging out with and what I was doing at work and pretty much everything that was going on in my life. We'd stay on the phone all night sometimes. I'd lie on my side with my phone on my ear, and we'd flip through channels, watching the same show or game on TV. Sometimes we'd stay on the phone until 3:00 a.m., or even 6:00 a.m.

There were so many things about her that naturally drew me to her. I was attracted to her physically, mentally, intellectually, and spiritually. She was the full package for me. I just wasn't ready to settle down when we first met.

The Biggest Decision in Life
When Laina threw that birthday party for me in 2005, I knew. I knew as clear as night and day. I had no doubt that she was the one. Now, for

the first time in my life, I was ready to fully commit everything I had to one woman.

One reason I knew this was that I had dated a lot, so I was clear about what I wanted and what I didn't want. I knew whom I naturally wanted to be with and whom I got tired of really quickly. In other relationships, the woman's physical beauty would fade in my eyes, and I was on to the next one. It never faded with my best friend.

The second reason was that I was always drawn to her. I knew that I couldn't live without her; I just couldn't. I knew that even if I married someone else, I would still want to call my best friend. I was that drawn to her. I finally knew what so many guys were talking about when they said they just "knew." I knew, and I couldn't deny it.

To say that I was excited would be a massive understatement. Marriage is one of the most important decisions anyone can make, if not *the* most important decision. The person you marry has an impact on your trajectory in life. It affects everything you do and who you become.

Don't settle! Be sure about what you want and why it matters to you. I've talked to a lot of people who've said that right before they got married, they'd gotten the feeling they should call it off. They failed to heed that feeling, and then suffered divorce down the road. You don't have to settle. You have a choice. If you're in a relationship right now that is not what you truly want, stop. Take a bold stand and fight for the relationship that you want.

Don't Settle

I was absolutely certain about whom I wanted to marry. When they say, "Marry your best friend," they're right. When I came to this decision, I bought a plane ticket and flew to Missouri so I could ask Laina's dad for permission to marry her.

In Missouri, I knocked on her parents' door and when her mom opened it, I sighed with relief. I was nervous about talking to her dad. I had spent time in their home before because I'd stayed there on my way to New England. I had visited her home with other friends and family members. But this was different; this time, I was asking for the greatest gift of my life.

Her dad soon came home, and I sat there with her parents and her aunt, who also lived there. I poured my heart out to him. I told him how much I loved his daughter, that she was my best friend, and that I wanted to marry her. I asked for his permission and blessing. He cried, her mom cried, and her aunt cried. And, of course, I cried. It was an unforgettable experience.

So that was it. I had permission. It was a quick trip, and I flew back the next morning. I got back on a Saturday and for the entire week, nothing happened. I knew I was going to propose; I just didn't know how and when. A week later, on Saturday morning, I knew it was the day. I called a bunch of our friends and told them to meet us at one of our favorite restaurants. I told my friends, "Today is the day!"

I kept the proposal simple. We'd always watched movies together; that was our thing. We went to one or two movies a week and we still do that today. A couple of days before this special day, we had gone to a movie and I was late because I was in a business meeting. Since this was before they had assigned seating in theaters, she was furious and didn't want to save my seat. She walked out of the theater, and we never watched the movie.

On the night I proposed, she drove down from Salt Lake, where she was living at the time. I told her we were going to a movie, and then I showed up late; that was part of the plan. When we got to the movies, I went in to get tickets and came back and fibbed, telling her that it was sold out. Laina was so angry I thought she might tell me the relationship was off. But I didn't sweat it; this was part of the night. On the drive home, she wouldn't even look at me or talk to me. She looked out the window the whole time.

She said, "Take me to my car. I'm going home."

I said, "Hey, let's just get a drink before we go."

She reluctantly agreed.

We went to Jamba Juice across from University Mall in Orem, Utah. This was the place where we'd had our first "date." When we got there, Laina was still upset with me. I knew it was time to reveal my plan.

With the ring in my pocket, I said, "Remember, this was where we had our first date almost five years ago to the day?"

She wasn't having it.

Then I got down on my knee in the parking lot and pulled out the ring.

I asked, "Will you marry me and be my wife forever?"

"Yes!" she exclaimed. Then she paused. "Hey, wait a minute," she said. "Are you doing this just because I'm mad?"

"Well, unless all of our friends are waiting for us at a nearby restaurant by coincidence, then no!" I replied.

We embraced each other and kissed and went into the restaurant to celebrate with our close friends.

It was a special time that I'll never forget. I knew what I wanted in my marriage, and I got it. I wanted a wife with whom I could be completely fulfilled, physically, spiritually, emotionally, and intellectually. I wanted my best friend.

Invest in Your Highest Priorities

Marriage can be powerful. Relationships are the source of our greatest joys in life. And that's why you should never settle. Dream about that person you want to be with for life. Write it all down and look back on it throughout the years. The woman I wrote about in my red journal in high school was independent, smart, beautiful, athletic, spiritual, and musical. I also wrote about having someone I could grow old with and lean on when I felt down. I got everything that I'd written about.

My wife has changed my life. She's my biggest supporter, and a shoulder I can lean on at all times. Even as I write this, I feel choked up inside.

You'll marry someone within your reach. If you, yourself, have grown in both mind-set and skill set, then you'll marry someone within that reach. They say you should become the type of person you want to marry. Instead of looking for Mr. or Mrs. "Right," become that person. It's true; I married up.

And when you do find that person, invest.

I invest in my highest priorities, and my wife is my highest priority. We go on date nights at least once a week, and sometimes twice a week. And yes, most of the time, it's still movies because that's what she loves. I do this because I know if I don't nurture my marriage, it will not grow.

This world is changing rapidly. In the face of distractions such as work, school, kids, church, workouts, sports, shopping, laundry, cleaning, and everything else, it's easy to neglect your marriage and not give it the time and energy it requires. It's easy to neglect family because you think they'll always be there. Infidelity destroys families and homes every day. Over the years, I've seen many marriages that have fallen apart. That's not what I want. I want to grow old with my wife. I'm committed to creating a hundred-plus years of happiness and joy in my marriage.

If you have made poor decisions in your marriage, course-correct immediately and begin rebuilding. If you're committed to it, and your spouse is committed to it, the marriage can work. But you've got to invest.

I love this interpretation by Matthew Henry:

Women were created from the rib of man to be beside him, not from his head to top him, nor from his feet to be trampled by him, but from under his arm to be protected by him, near to his heart to be loved by him.

Men, rise up and honor your wives. Women, have the courage to confront your husbands when necessary and to support and love them. A wife knows her husband better than anyone. My wife knows me the best, and has the ability to make me believe I can do the impossible. She also knows how to stop me cold me in my tracks. I am grateful that she is a strong woman who helps me to be the best I can be.

Here are some of my must-dos for a successful marriage. I don't just teach these principles to my clients; I live them. They are powerful when lived. And while Pinterest, Instagram, and Facebook are full of cute quotes about marriage, cute quotes don't empower marriages. **A sincere commitment to doing what is required is what empowers a marriage.**

- Take your spouse on a weekly date. If you travel, then take your spouse out when you are home. Consistency is the key in the beginning. Leave the kids at home with a sitter and go to dinner or a movie, or just drive someplace and sit in the car and talk and kiss. Be present with each other. Listen intently when your spouse is talking. Date night is for connecting and rekindling your passion as a couple, and for being a couple without having to be parents. Weekly date night is NONNEGOTIABLE.

- Go on at least one getaway each year. That means leaving your kids at home and traveling to another location. Spend three or four days alone together, talking, making love, joking, playing games, and being present with each other. If you can, do this twice a year—and four times a year is better. Time away is also nonnegotiable.

- Pray together often, and hold hands when you pray. Pray for each other and for your kids. Thank God aloud for your spouse.

- Listen to each other. Put your phone away and be present in the moment. Create "blackout" periods in which there are no electronics on and it's pure family time.
- Send daily messages of love, honor, and appreciation. Send these through video, text, audio, e-mail, handwritten notes, and dry-erase marker on bathroom mirrors. These daily messages build love and trust.
- Buy flowers or shoes for your spouse, or whatever he or she values. Do this spontaneously and regularly. We have a dozen or so Kobe Bryant shoes on our shoe rack, and I'm sure there will be more.
- Talk about everything: Intimacy, sex, money, jobs, work, kids, your ideal home, vacations, what you like, what you don't like, religion, spirituality, etc. Honesty is crucial, and most couples don't talk about the crucial things. Tell the truth.
- Touch each other affectionately. Hold hands, kiss, hug, and cuddle. Do this daily. Treat each other like you did when you were first dating, when you couldn't keep your hands off each other. Show your kids that this is what married people do and how great it is.
- Express heartfelt appreciation and love on a daily basis. Water what you want to grow.
- Rub your spouse's feet, legs, back, and any other part of the body that makes him or her feel great. Consistently demonstrate the extent of your love and adoration through both words and actions.
- Have date nights where you dress up in fancy clothes and go out on the town. This breaks the routine of the weekly date night, preventing it from becoming boring.
- Serve each other selflessly. My wife loves when I rub her feet. I love having delicious meals cooked by my wife. I also love the

little notes she leaves in my bags when I travel, and when she just comes up behind me and kisses me while I'm working.

- Have those conversations that can be difficult and scary. Conflict and confrontation are healthy if you both remember you're on the same team.

- Set aside a weekly time to talk and take inventory of what's going on, what's working, what's not working, and how to improve. Great winning teams and companies do this; why not *your* team?

- Don't settle for a mediocre or good marriage. Strive for a *great* marriage. Confront problems and deal with them.

- Have open communication 24/7. No hiding, no pretending, no suppressing—give each other permission to talk, vent, and express the complete truth. When one person is talking, the other listens. If one of you needs space, create rules that will provide for that.

- If your spouse stays home, give him or her the opportunity to get out and about. My wife goes to play ball twice a week in a league, and it's just me and the boys at home. She gets time to do what she wants and comes home recharged and energized.

- Allow your spouse to have her own bank account with her own money to spend freely without guilt or worry. (I'm speaking to those men who are entrepreneurs and have wives who stay home.)

- Weather the storms. There will be times when you'll be tempted to look elsewhere and stray from the commitments and vows you made. Commit to staying the course and working through any conflicts that could destroy what you have. What you focus on will expand. What you focus on is what you'll feel. What you focus on grows. Focus on your spouse.

I love my wife deeply. She is my goddess, and while some laugh and poke fun at me for calling her my goddess, it's truly how I feel. Long ago, I realized I'd be miserable if I based my actions on pleasing other people and worrying about their personal projections of their lives onto mine. Do not allow other people to run or ruin your marriage. After all, pulling other people down doesn't enable you to go higher; it just pulls other people down.

Do not settle. If your marriage is struggling now, fight for it. And if you say, "Well, we'll stay together for the kids," who are you kidding? Showing your children that marriage has to be painful and unhappy is doing them and you a disservice. And if you've done all you can in fighting for your marriage and it's not going anywhere, then have the courage to do whatever is necessary to move your lives forward powerfully.

I believe most marriages can work out if both spouses are willing to fight to preserve the marriage. This may require real forgiveness and love, and for some marriages, time to heal from the past. There are always ups and downs in a marriage. There's nothing wrong with a little spice and fire in a marriage, either. I wanted a wife who wouldn't be dependent on me, who was strong enough to lead me if I forgot my role. I love my goddess.

Questions to Consider Carefully and Answer:

- On a scale of 1 to 10, 1 being horrific and 10 being awesome, rate your marriage in terms of:
  - Communication (how often and how well you communicate)
  - Intimacy (frequency and enjoyment of physical touch and sex)

- ○ Enjoyment (being around each other and overall happiness together)
- ○ Service (how often you do things for each other)
- What would it take to reach 10 in each of those categories?
- If it's at 10 already, how can you help other couples get to 10?
- What stops you from taking your spouse out on a weekly date? If you already do, do you have variety or has date night become boring and routine?
- What would allow your sex and intimacy to become great again if it's died down?
- What would it take to reignite the fire and passion in your marriage?
- Do you want to stay married to your spouse?
- What one thing could you do today that would make a drastic difference in your marriage?
- What message does how you treat your spouse send to your children about marriage and family?
- Have you settled for a marriage that doesn't meet your needs? Don't settle!

CHAPTER 10

Wilderness and Despair
What You Don't Know or Don't Admit Will Destroy You

| ı ı ı ı ı | ı ı ı ı ı | ı ı ı ı ı | ı ı ı ı ı | ı ı ı ı ı | ı ı ı ı ı | ı ı ı ı ı

"You have to take risks. We will only understand the miracle
of life fully when we allow the unexpected to happen."
—Paulo Coelho

I n the late spring of 2007, I got a phone call that struck fear into my heart: "Hey, you just lost half a million dollars with this thing down in Florida."

I thought to myself, *Not a big deal. I've still got other resources that I can work with.*

But I was wrong. Dead wrong.

Slowly, everything that my family had money in started to dry up. February 2008 was even worse. I fought to keep my head above water, but I knew I wouldn't be able to pay the overhead on all the properties, businesses, leases, and people when the first of the month rolled around again.

This wasn't my reality yet, but the story I'd created in my own mind—essentially, that the sky was falling—caused so much stress I couldn't sleep. I thought March 1 would be the worst day of my life because I'd be unable to pay. And then March 1 came and went and nothing happened. It was just another day. But there was still trouble on the horizon, and it had all started a few years prior.

In 2006, we had more money than we knew what to do with. I had just purchased a Mercedes-Benz AMG S65 and had spent another $15,000 on the engine, bumping me up to 700 horses in this beautiful summer sedan. It was a $200,000 car, and I was throwing money around like it was candy in a parade.

I bought my wife a brand-new Range Rover, and six months later, I bought myself a new Cadillac Escalade. I was ignorant and frivolous with my money back then because I thought it was never going to go away. I remember lying down one night with our newborn son between us.

My wife asked, "Do you think God's going to take everything away from us to teach us some lessons?"

"If He does, we'll just get it all back," I said. I was overconfident.

Two and half years later, the repo man knocked on my door and I handed him the keys to my Mercedes. Four months later, I handed them the keys to my wife's Range Rover. In November of that same year, we handed them the keys to the Escalade, only a week before getting evicted from our home in Provo, Utah. Our long journey into the wilderness was just beginning.

It's natural to want to avoid the wilderness and the challenging times, but it's during those dark times that you get tested. As I mentioned earlier in the book, it's then that you question if God is there and wonder if anything is going to work out. These are the times that are most crucial for our growth, and we can grow if we embrace adversity.

Cancer? The death of a young child or a spouse? Financial turmoil? Unexpected tragedy? These experiences give us perspective if we humble ourselves enough to see it.

When my wife asked, "Do you think God's going to take everything away from us to teach us some lessons?" I had no idea what was coming. There are challenges that are divinely customized for our growth and progression, and there are challenges that are self-imposed. Whether my troubles arose because God was testing me or because of my own poor choices, those troubles enabled me to grow.

If you respond to adversity by looking immediately to God and asking, "Why are you punishing me, God?" it may be time to step back and ask, "How did I create this situation in the first place?" If we're unwise stewards of our resources, we'll reap the natural consequences of our foolish business decisions. Owning up to the consequences of your actions is one of the first steps for gaining power in your life. It's called extreme ownership.

The reality was, I was reckless with our money. I felt invincible, as though I couldn't do wrong. I bought homes left and right. If I made a poor decision, I didn't think it was big deal. I'd just make more money to cover up the errors. I thought it would last forever. I thought I was untouchable.

If you don't stay relevant and innovative in the marketplace, you'll lose big. You'll become obsolete, which is what happened to Blockbuster. If you don't question what's going on with your resources, then you should not expect to win. If you believe you're untouchable, and fail to act with humility, it is unlikely that you will succeed, whatever your endeavor.

"Pride goeth before destruction, and a haughty spirit before a fall."[2] My fall was just beginning.

---

2   Proverbs 16:18

Storytelling

When I think about that fateful time in the spring of 2008, and how I worried myself almost to death about not being able to pay our overhead and payroll, I realize it was all a story I made up—a big, fat lie.

We make up stories and lies in almost everything we do. How often do we suffer unnecessary anxiety over things we cannot control? I couldn't control the economy, and yet, I would stress out about it. The stress resulted not from what was happening, but from my *thoughts* about what was happening. In your life, when you begin to feel stress, frustration, or anxiety, look at your thoughts about "what is." Stress and frustration come from your beliefs about reality. Byron Katie, author of one of my favorite books, *Loving What Is*, says when we argue with reality, we lose … and more than losing, we suffer.

If you find yourself stressed about anything right now, ask yourself, *What story am I telling right now that is causing this stress?*

Another powerful question you can ask yourself is, *What is it within me that causes me to want to choose* stress?"

Stress, frustration, anxiety, and other unnecessary feelings come because we choose them. I've seen this in my clients and myself: We are addicted to stress. We are addicted to worrying.

We are also addicted to drama. The way you choose stress is by focusing on things you cannot control and then making up a story about them. This is similar to how children make up stories about monsters in the dark: Monsters aren't real, but because children *think* they're real, they feel frightened, and then behaviors follow the feelings. If you want to save yourself from stress, anxiety, frustration, or anger, challenge your thoughts about "what is." When I stress out about anything, it's almost always because of the story I am telling and the meaning I am attaching to it—neither of which is real. Here are a few examples of this principle:

- You're the boss of a company and payroll is coming up. You realize cash flow is tight and you're unsure how to make it through this month.
  Made-up story: *We're falling apart and the world is going to end.*
  Feelings: *Frustration, stress, anger*
  What's really happening: *Cash flow is tight.*

- You're a sales manager and have built a great team. Managers from other organizations continually recruit your well-trained reps.
  Made-up story: *Your reps don't appreciate you and all you've done, and the managers taking your reps are dishonest and shady.*
  Feelings: *Anger, frustration, stress, hate, sadness*
  What's really happening: *Your reps see another opportunity and they're going for it.*

- You're a parent with children ages four, six, eight, and twelve. They are normal kids. They argue, laugh, use the cushions as punching bags, leave the milk out, and do all the things normal kids do. One day, they drop the milk on the floor and it goes everywhere.
  Made-up story: *Kids never listen. They don't appreciate you; they're disobedient and disrespectful. What's wrong with them?*
  Feelings: *Frustration, anger, stress, victimhood*
  What's really happening: *The kids spilled the milk.*

In each of these examples, the individual makes up an unnecessary story about "what is," and these made-up stories cause frustration, anger, sadness, and feelings of victimhood. It doesn't have to be this way. I highly recommend Byron Katie's book *Loving What Is* for detailed training on this subject.

When I began to lose everything in 2008, I was in "make-up mode." The stories I made up included: *God is punishing me. I'm not a good businessman. I have to be tested and tried.* The reality? *The economy was turning and many mortgage and real estate professionals were getting hammered. We weren't prepared for it. I wasn't prepared for it.*

By the middle of March 2008, my phone started to blow up with creditors looking for their money. I was getting thirty to forty calls a day at a minimum. My phone wouldn't stop ringing. Properties started to foreclose. Cars began to get notices. By November, we'd lost the Escalade. I remember taking a picture of the car, thinking, *One day, this is going to be a great story.* Indeed, it has been more than a great story. It's been a blockbuster movie. And this is how you must look at your life. When you go through bad times, just know it's going to be a great movie, a great story to tell, and something you can look back on and say, "We overcame it."

After the Escalade went, we didn't have a car, so my good friend Jake lent me his truck. I went from having three cars, a big house, a sweet office, and a number of properties to no cars, no properties, and getting ready to be kicked out of my home. Jake had nothing either, yet he gave me his truck to use. I was so grateful. Another friend of mine, José let me use his Audi for nearly six months. He did this, he said, because years earlier, I had helped to save his life with a phone call. Because I had made a difference in his life, he wanted to help me out.

Before we got kicked out of our home, another friend of mine, Kelly, told me he had a house in Highland, Utah, that was going into foreclosure in four months, and that we could move into it for a while. It was Thanksgiving. My family came down, helped us pack up our home, and helped us move. Shortly thereafter, I sold my wife's wedding ring to put gas in the car and food on the table. It was time to do some searching.

Through this difficult time of losing material possessions, I realized in a profound way that friendships and relationships matter. My family and friends are extremely important to me. They have been there for me in difficult times, and I strive to be there for them when they need me.

Who are your friends? Can you count on them? Who are your colleagues? Would they be there for you if you needed them? Can you count on them to help you as some of my friends did for me? Can they count on you if they need you? Make a point of nurturing these relationships, because when it comes down to it, they will be there when everything else is gone.

Selling the Super Bowl Ring

In 2009, we were living in Highland, Utah, in a home that we had no business living in, and I was trying to figure out our next move.

"You said you'd do anything for our family," my wife said. "Are you going to sell your Super Bowl ring?"

I was stunned. How could she ask me to do this? Was she out of her mind? This wasn't just a ring. It was something I had worked hard to earn. Now my wife wanted me to sell it?

I was embarrassed and ashamed, but she was right. At the same time, I had an inner drive that led me to believe that I would get the ring back eventually. So I found a collector and we made the deal. I bought a ticket to New York City and my wife drove me to the airport. I cried the whole way there. I couldn't believe it. I was angry. How could this have happened?

At that time, we were on EBT—code for food stamps. I tried to build a business, but nothing worked. I was in "cheap" mode. I attempted to build without real certainty and guidance. I tried to bootstrap my business, watching videos and reading e-books, and trying to launch a legitimate company. **This is the fastest way to lose money and go broke.**

Think about this: My goal was to produce a seven-figure business that year, and I thought I could do it without any real investment or guidance from mentors or consultants. I thought I could do it by reading e-books and watching free online training videos. I was delusional, as are many so-called "entrepreneurs" in today's marketplace who think that "likes" on Facebook and followers on Snapchat equal money.

In hindsight, of course I'd do it differently. If you're going to build a business, the cheap route will be the most expensive route in the long run. So don't do it. The greatest thing I could have done back then would have been hire a mentor, pay him some big money, and keep investing in myself. It's silly to think that in 2009 I thought I would build a cash-producing business without investing time, energy, and money. The fact is, I didn't have the skill set or mind-set to build any business. The mortgage industry had exposed me because although I thought I was skilled, I'd only been riding the momentum of trends in the marketplace.

If you're not making money, you're not creating value in the marketplace. And if you think you have real value to offer and are still not making money, there is a flaw somewhere in your skills, mind-set, marketing, or sales. I'll say this again because it's important: **If I had to do it again, I would have paid a coach or mentor to help me build my business, plain and simple.**

If you're committed to building a legitimate, cash-earning business that's sustainable and predictable, then plan on investing serious time, energy, and money. There's no way around it. You start where you are and invest in yourself.

Here are four ways to invest in yourself and your business:

1. Invest in mentors, coaches, and/or consultants to guide you through the pitfalls. This is a must. A great coach will help you see what you cannot see and help you to get to the root problems that stop you from getting what you want. If you cannot invest directly in a mentor, go work for one and learn from him or her.

2. Invest in your employees for their training, growth, and expansion. Your employees are your number one customers. Take care of them and they will take care of you and your company.

3. Invest in proper systems and technology to run an efficient and effective business. Can you imagine if Apple were trying to conduct business using its computers from ten years ago? It wouldn't work. Keep up with technology, systems, and processes and stay relevant in the conversation or you may become extinct.

4. Invest in your marketing and sales to grow your clientele and bottom-line cash. Have a daily love affair with marketing, and treat it like you would treat your spouse or significant other. Solid businesses invest in marketing to stay relevant in their industries. Marketing looks different for every business, so find what works for you and commit to it.

Invest in your business the same way you invest in your marriage, family, health, and spirituality. Put time, energy, attention, and resources into it so that it will grow and flourish.

When you focus, invest, and do the required work, the returns will come. Even if they don't come immediately, they will eventually show up. If you think you're going to bootstrap your company into a multimillion- or billion-dollar operation, you have a very long and difficult road ahead of you. Anything of value requires a significant investment and a sincere commitment.

The year 2009 came and went. All the money I'd gotten from the sale of my Super Bowl ring was gone, and I was still trying to figure something out. By 2010, I knew that we weren't going to get out of the situation, so I filed for bankruptcy that summer. I stood before the judge feeling embarrassed and humiliated. How had I gone from the NFL to mortgage and real estate millions to bankruptcy?

I was extremely depressed and very overweight. I even had suicidal thoughts for a moment. It's crazy to me now that I felt that way, but it was real. It was so depressing to be on the bottom. Most "gurus" won't share the real truth with you: that they know what it's like to fail big or to have to start over with nothing. I've learned that in a marketplace full of people who don't always tell the truth or the whole truth, those who are fastest to be real and raw, win.

Some of the greatest lessons I've learned came from that difficult experience. When you face resistance, keep going. You must be focused on and dedicated to achieving your dreams. If you simply sit back and assume that the world will make them come true for you, you will wind up deeply disappointed. The world has another job to do and it will do it: It will deliver tests to see if you're serious about what you say you want.

The Power of Your Word

I needed to draw a line in the sand and walk away, and I did. The million-plus dollars of investment money I'd raised from family, close friends, and private investors had disappeared with the mortgage and real estate meltdown. I gave these people my word that I would pay them back no matter how long it took. I'm not worried about it because I know I will take care of them. How do I know? Because I gave my word. Your word matters. My word matters. When you know you can follow through on commitments no matter what, the universe moves to help you. When you know you are your word, you have the greatest power to produce, to overcome adversity, and to pick yourself up, regardless of circumstance.

I can already see the day when I will write each one of these people a check for the amount they invested in me. Does it matter that I made no money on their investment? Not at all. They knew it was a risk because any investment requires a degree of risk, but I gave them my word and that is that.

Visualize yourself overcoming whatever you're facing right now in your life. If you're deep in debt, visualize yourself producing massive profit either in your current business or in a new business, and envision how great it will feel to pay off that debt. If you've struggled with weight or a health issue, visualize yourself on TV telling the story of how you overcame it, while inspiring hundreds of thousands of people with your story. If you're recently divorced, imagine what it will feel like to be in your ideal relationship with a person who adores you and with whom you connect with on deep levels of trust, love, and intimacy.

The ability to see it first in one's mind is critical. I teach this to my sons by having them finish a phrase: I say, "See it first …" and they answer, "… in my mind."

I imagine being at a nice restaurant, enjoying a fine dinner conversation with each of the families to whom I owe money, and sharing with them how much they mean to me and what the previous years have been like. I see myself presenting an envelope to each one of those families with the amount of money they invested in me. I can *see* it. That vision inspires me and drives me to stay committed to my purpose, my passion, and my path. Do it. It works.

This period in my life was one of the most difficult I have ever faced. We sold everything we owned. But I still had my wife and my son, and during this challenging time, our second son was born. I saw God's hands in our lives and felt His tender mercies throughout this journey. I saw and felt the blessings. Even though we had little money, we had sufficient funds for our needs. I learned to trust Him no matter what. I didn't realize it at the time, but these challenging years laid the foundation and stoked the fire for me to prosper again in a very big way, much bigger than I ever could have imagined.

Could I ever get out of this rut that I was in? Only if I chose to.

Can you get out of the deep, dark ruts you are currently in? Only if you choose to.

Questions to Consider Carefully and Answer:

- What story that does not serve you are you telling today about a current circumstance?
- What new story can you begin to tell about your circumstance that would empower you rather than drag you down?
- How are your adversities self-imposed?
- What would your life look like if you chose to get out of your own way?
- How does adversity affect your mind-set?
- What skills are you lacking that prevent you from achieving your desired results?
- Are you willing to do what's required to change your life?

CHAPTER 11

What's Old Is New Again
Rediscovering the Grind

|ıııı|ıııı|ıııı|ıııı|ıııı|ıııı|ıııı

"Some people dream of success, while others wake up and work hard at it."
—Winston Churchill

I t was almost 10:00 p.m. I was walking in a neighborhood in Hephzibah, Georgia. My shirt was soaked with sweat from a long day of knocking on doors in that Southern humidity. My car group was late in picking me up; one of my guys must have been in an after-hours sales meeting. I made it a habit to walk the streets of my neighborhood with my iPad, looking for anyone who might be home whom I had missed earlier in the day.

As I walked up and down these streets, I approached a mother and her son out on a late-night walk. I recognized the son because I'd knocked on their door multiple times in the past week, and his mom was never home. This lady who couldn't have stood taller than five-foot-four glared at me, seeing me only in the dim light of my iPad.

"What are you doing out here so late?" she asked.

I asked her the same question.

Then I explained, "I haven't talked to you yet." I introduced myself and told her that we needed to go to her home so I could show her what I was doing. It was now 10:30 p.m.

Over the next thirty minutes, I sold her a home-automation system. My technician showed up at 11:15 p.m. and I walked outside while he installed it for her. Sixty percent of her neighbors' homes had been broken into, and 75 percent of them had some type of security, such as dogs, bars on windows, or lights around their home. These people needed to feel safe in their homes. And I had a solution.

It had started three months earlier. I had just arrived home from New Zealand after having spent thirty days down there with a network marketing company. I was in a group that allowed me to build fast and make good money quickly. But it wasn't the money that I was used to making, and I wanted to make more money, faster. I was overweight and deeply depressed, but I continued to smile, push forward, and give it my all. I needed something that could give me real confidence and a financial boost.

After returning from New Zealand at the end of February 2011, I'd met one of my old friends who had been trying to recruit me for the last two years. I told him what I was doing, and he said he wanted to meet again. So I met him at the Happy Sumo in Provo. As he had done previously, he strongly encouraged me to come work for a company called Vivint, recruiting sales reps, managing a team, and doing door-to-door sales.

The two previous times he had tried to recruit me, I had been confident in what I was doing and uninterested in the offer. Each year he'd show me his 1099, which doubled in size from one year to the next. It was a ridiculous amount of money and I was happy for him, but I'd already had my own thing going on the first two times we sat down.

But something was different this time around. By 2011, I had been humbled. I had nothing significant going for me businesswise. I was disheartened and unsure about the direction of my life and the welfare of my wife and two sons. I was getting used to just "getting by," and the successful years of 2004 through 2007 were a distant memory.

Casey Baugh was one of the kindest and most confident men I knew.

He said, "I think you'd absolutely kill it. I think you'd do well, and this would help to launch you into what you really want to do"—which was to coach, teach, train, and speak. Yes, C-Baugh (as I call him) knew what I wanted and saw a way to help me get it. In the process, he saw that I could help him grow his team and his future.

He asked me one question that changed everything: "How much do you need to make this summer for this to be worth it?"

Oh, the power of questions. I had a number in my mind, but I was almost embarrassed to say it because I wasn't sure it could be done.

When I told him the amount, he slapped the table and said, "Done! You can make that, but this is what it's going to take."

For the next forty-five minutes, he told me how I was going to have to hustle hard, and that it wouldn't be easy.

"You're going to have to work harder than you've ever worked. If you treat this like you treated football, you can make that amount of money in the next four or five months."

I kept asking questions and he kept answering them. Then he gave me the blueprint, and I adopted it to a T. I took notes ferociously on the brown paper that covered our table at the sushi house. I ripped the paper off, put it in my journal, and went home to tell my wife what I was contemplating doing. To my surprise, she was all for it. I couldn't believe it! Perhaps it was because we had been struggling for nearly four years, after having enjoyed massive prosperity in the years before that. My business inadequacies caused pain to my wife, but she was nonetheless strong and supportive through those struggling years of growth.

I was preparing to completely shift gears and knock on doors as a door-to-door salesman, when previously I had been a successful mortgage banker, teacher, speaker, trainer, and Super Bowl champion. This was a job I'd looked down upon and thought I was too good to do. More than that, it was a job I was afraid to do. What if I failed? What if I couldn't hack it? I've said it before and I'll say it again: God has a way of teaching you valuable lessons in the furnace of adversity, and if you're humble and open to receiving those divine gifts, you'll receive them.

The Master Recruiter

I took my wife to C-Baugh's home—his beautiful, brand-new home in a very wealthy neighborhood.

She looked at him, then looked at me, and said to me convincingly, "You can do this. You should go and sell."

If you ever want to recruit a husband to do a job, recruit his wife. That's what C-Baugh did with me. He has to be as good a recruiter as some of the great college coaches of today like Urban Meyer, Nick Saban, Kalani Sitake, and Jim Harbaugh.

C-Baugh became my mentor and coach over the next few years. If he said it, it was doctrine. I have reams of notes on everything he told me to do. When he spoke, I listened; I took notes and then applied his instructions to my work. I still look back on those notes occasionally to remind myself of the sacrifices we made in those early knocking days. They were glorious days.

"This will be one of the hardest things you'll ever do, Setema." His words kept running through my mind. For a man who's been at the top before, those words were the music of the Pied Piper. I couldn't help but want to do the job. C-Baugh knew that my fear and hesitancy were normal.

"Why don't you just watch one of the sales being conducted? Just go look. Don't make a four-month decision. Just watch and decide."

The Doors of Opportunity

We drove to Idaho with very little money in our bank account. I took my wife and two sons with me; that's how we rolled then, and it's still how I roll. If I go somewhere, they come with me.

I went to watch a sales trainer to see if this job was something I could see myself doing. The whole time, I was nervous, wondering if I could do this job. Could I sell door to door? With every tribulation you face, there is an opportunity to grow, but my confidence was at an all-time low. Since losing everything in 2008, I hadn't really tasted success, so any victories, however small, were to be celebrated and appreciated.

We got to Idaho and checked into the cheapest hotel I could find. I had a sales manual the size of a phone book. A short, powerful, funny guy named Dan Tracy picked me up, and off we went to see if this knocking deal was doable for me.

I hadn't felt this uncomfortable in a long time. He knocked on doors; people answered. He was as smooth as James Bond. Within one minute, he was in the house, telling me to follow him inside. It was almost as if he'd barged his way in, or at least that's how it appeared to me. But this great man showed me what was possible. His example changed my family's life.

I watched the customers as Dan talked. At first, it seemed that they were irritated with us, but it didn't affect my trainer. It was as if he couldn't see it. He went about his business of selling, and showing them the benefits of the system. If they didn't take it, he'd try again. I couldn't believe how easy it was for him to get into a home. Although he was half my size, this commanding Idaho cowboy was as bold as a lion. He was funny and made selling enjoyable while showing me the ropes. Of course, I projected discomfort because that's how I viewed everything. Homeowners kept telling him no, but he blew through their smoke screens like Kobe Bryant driving through defenders for an easy dunk.

The third house was a perfect candidate. Their home had been broken into and they were quickly on board. Dan sold them everything, from cameras to door locks to window sensors. It was frightening to hear this lady's recollection of someone crawling onto her roof and entering her home. Dan did everything that was in the book and had me fill out the paperwork. He took a picture of me making my first deal. He was the perfect trainer, full of encouragement and humor; he was a real fireball.

When he dropped me off at the hotel that night, he said, "I'll see you at 9:00 tomorrow morning."

My wife asked how it had gone.

I said, "I don't know, but I'll never know until I try." I told her about Dan and his savvy salesmanship, and then I stayed up till 1:00 a.m. studying the manual. I woke up early and continued studying.

When Dan picked me up to knock, it was freezing. Even though it was March, it was still snowing. We entered the first home again with no problem. I began to see the things I'd studied the night before. The family didn't buy, but we were on to the next house.

At the next door, he said, "It's your turn." I'm sure he saw the fear on my face, but he said, "You can do it. I'll be right behind you."

When the homeowner came to the door, I fumbled my words, but Dan guided me. We got in the door and I fumbled through the pitch. The homeowner didn't buy.

After that, he said, "Well, it's time to spread your wings and fly. That's the only way you're going to learn."

I was horrified, but I knew he was right. I was there to see if I could do this job so I could get out of the financial rut I was in.

Off I went, knocking door to door. I made it into a couple of homes but got rejected most of the time. At the end of the day, I called my wife and told her to pick me up.

I got into the car, and, with certainty and poise, told her, "I can do this. I know I can do it." I felt a killer instinct and hunger I hadn't felt in almost four years. The competitive part of me began to come out again. I wanted to be the top rookie that year. Some say competition is bad, and the only person you should compete against is yourself. While that may serve some, I chose that year to compete against others and it worked.

Burning the Ships

My family and I flew out to Hawaii so I could deliver a keynote address alongside recording artist Jack Johnson, renowned chef Sam Choy, and a few other local celebrities. This was the last time my family and I would be together until June. A couple of weeks later, I kissed my wife and kids good-bye and boarded on a plane to South Carolina. The plan was for my wife to pack up our home and drive out in June. I flew out early to get the ball rolling and figure out the business. I couldn't believe I was doing this job, or that being a door-to-door salesman was my life now. I didn't realize I was embarking on a journey that would forever change my life, more than any seminar or book ever could.

When I got to South Carolina, I was more committed than ever. I had read a story about a sixteenth-century Spanish conquistador by the name of Hernán Cortés. Cortés and his small group of soldiers and sailors landed on the shores of the part of the New World now known as Mexico, in a dozen or so ships. They were far from their homeland, thousands of miles across the Atlantic Ocean. Their purpose was to conquer the locals—the Aztecs—and rob them of their fortune. After Cortés had his men unload the ships, they rested and examined the land. As they prepared to hike, he had a few men burn their own ships.

Some of the men shouted, "The enemy knows we are here. Our ships are on fire!"

Cortés replied, "I burned the ships because without them, there is no way of sailing back to the motherland. We either conquer this land or we die, and the only way we go back to our land is on *their* ships. We conquer or die."

It worked. His small force conquered all of Mexico and established a Spanish empire in the New World that lasted several hundred years. This was how I felt. There was no going back for me now. There was no retreat; I had burned my ships. This was my do-or-die situation, and I wasn't going to die.

I knew what my *why* was. After you know *what* you want, the next step is to have a *why* backing it up. I had a big *why*. I was tired of being financially mediocre. I was tired of not prospering. I was fed up with not having the life we truly wanted and I was sick and tired of scraping the bottom of the barrel. I knew I had a mission to fulfill, and remaining in poverty had no part of it. The great pain forced me to alter my thinking and behaviors.

Do you have a *why* for your life? Your *why* is your holy cause. It will drive you to do things you'd never do otherwise. Find your *why*. Create your *why*. Choose your *why*. It could be your family, your highest purpose, God, your religion, fame, riches, or anything you choose. As Jim Rohn says, "The bigger the *why*, the easier the *how*." I had my *why*.

I had very little money when I arrived in South Carolina. I didn't realize that I needed to buy my own sheets, blankets, pillows, and food. This was very humbling for me. I barely had enough money to buy food, but my ships had been burned and it was time to go to work. The next morning, I showed up to the first sales meeting of the knocking season.

It was crazy. It was like a locker room before a game. Music was blasting while forty-plus reps talked and prepped themselves to knock. I didn't know anyone except the manager. A lot of the guys had sales experience, but I made up my mind that I was going to be the number-one salesman in the room. I was going to beat everyone, including the manager and the third- and fourth-year reps. It was go time.

Relentless Commitment

C-Baugh had given me the recipe. Sell twelve to fifteen a week—two to three a day, and four to five on Saturdays. Hustle and grind. Work the hours. Be relentless. Simple, yet difficult. That first meeting was led by our manager, Brandon Holmes. I sat in the back with the attitude of "Y'all dudes don't stand a chance. I will outwork and outsell every one of you guys this year." That killer instinct was waking up inside me. I began channeling a fierce fury at life. When you're in a state of apathy, anger is the best remedy—and I had been asleep for a few years. But now I was angry.

My first area was an hour away from our apartments. I was nervous, but this was it. I had failed miserably over the past few years, but now it was time to be present, here in South Carolina. I had no experience filling out paperwork. I didn't know what I was doing; all I could do was what I had observed Dan Tracy doing weeks earlier. That first day, I got dropped off and began to knock relentlessly. I knocked and knocked. I was let into homes. I tried and didn't stop walking, knocking, and talking. I'd made a commitment to my wife that I would be as relentless and committed as anyone on the planet had ever been. I knew I needed to get a sale on my first day. I had to do it. It was a must.

The sun started to set and my heart began racing with urgency. I had been so close on a couple of deals but couldn't get them to pull the trigger. I was optimistic that I would find someone willing to buy. As it got dark, around 9:00, my car group began to text me, asking, "Where are you?" I ignored them. I'd interviewed some of the best salesmen and they'd all said, "Knock late and sell late." This was also what C-Baugh had told me. I couldn't believe I hadn't sold anything yet.

It was pitch black outside. I knew I was knocking on my last door of the day.

A guy with a Boston accent opened the door and asked, "What you doing out here so late?"

I had a "Hail Mary" mind-set because I knew this was my last door of the day. I had nothing to lose. I was bold and asked to see his current security panel. Once he let me in, it was over and I knew it. I showed him how everything worked, and by 10:30, he was sold. I had no idea how to fill out the paperwork or do the closing call. One of the reps from my car group walked in and filled it out for me. The deal was done; I'd made the sale.

I was so happy and excited. More than that, I was grateful. I'd walked, knocked, and talked all day. I'd had no idea how gratifying a sale could be. We got home close to midnight that night. I knelt down in my living room with no lights on and I cried in prayer to God. I was so grateful. I called my wife and shared our success. I lay down on the couch and fell asleep with my contacts in and without showering. My mind and body were exhausted.

The next morning, I woke up super early to shower, study, and prep for the day. I knocked, talked, and walked all day without any results. Then I knocked on the door of the neighbor who lived next to my sale the night before, and I got my second sale. The husband was a soldier deployed overseas, and this mother of three was always worried about her children and their home. It was just what she was seeking.

I went on to learn the mind-sets and skill sets necessary to be a successful door-to-door salesman. Few understood my drive or why I worked harder than anyone. But I understood that in order to make a difference with selling, I needed to collapse time. There were two differences between me and the other salesmen who were making a lot of money:

1. **Skill set** (which came from time on the doors and focused, intense practice)
2. **Mind-set** (how I viewed myself and the world)

The only differences between you as you are now and the you that could produce ten to one hundred times more in business are skill set and mind-set.

Collapsing Time

The top managers were making a healthy six figures as leaders. I was a rookie committed to cracking those numbers. The veterans of the industry had practiced for hours upon hours and refined their skill sets over days, weeks, months, and years. I committed to collapsing time. I had a simple plan: I'd memorize the scripts, practice and role-play, learn to overcome every objection, and outwork everyone in the whole country.

The way it worked was old-school hustle and grind. I got up at 6:00 every morning. I studied for about two and a half hours. From the time I woke up, the training would play on my speakers in my apartment. My walls were covered with big, sticky sheets of paper from Staples that had all my notes and reminders on them. As soon as I got out of bed, I pressed "play." If I was using the bathroom, I was listening to training. If I was showering, I was listening to training. If I was cooking, I was listening to training. I'd listen over and over to the best of the best, so I could understand the mind-set of these guys. Vivint had created powerful sales videos of some of the top reps in the industry, and I must have watched and listened to each video at least a hundred times. It was similar to watching game film. The great athletes study film and create mental pictures of what success must look like.

I created a powerful real-time affirmation based on my friend Ann Web's *Ideal LifeVision*, which involves speaking in the first person in a positive, present-tense, as if you've already done the thing you want to do. You record it and listen to it daily. I spoke my goals into a recorder in detail and played Baroque music in the background. I listened to that every day. This is what I wrote, spoke, and listened to that summer:

> *I'm the number one rookie of 2011. I sell over two hundred accounts by December. I master the art of sales. People love me. Everyone loves Setema. People are waiting for Setema to knock on their door and provide value and service to them. I outwork everyone; no one works harder than I do. No one studies harder than I do. I knock early. I knock late. I'm a beast on the doors. I draw nearer to my God, who leads me each day. My wife and my sons are depending on me to bring home food for them. I'm the hardest working, most relentless salesman in the world. I overcome objections easily and sell effortlessly. People buy from me. I sell my first account before 4:00 p.m. I sell my second account before 6:00 p.m. I sell my third account before 7:30 p.m. I always sell an account after 8:00 p.m. I dominate Saturdays. I sell at least four on Saturdays.*

I listened to that and repeated that every day of 2011. I took notes relentlessly during correlation meetings. I carried my training manuals and all my notes with me everywhere. We typically drove an hour to knocking areas, and I studied the whole way there. I was a studying and practicing machine. Other reps would sleep and talk, or listen to music. I didn't have time to sleep or listen to music. I didn't have time for movies or small talk. I was broke and I needed to cut the learning curve in half, and do it *now*. For some guys, this was a fun opportunity. For them, it was just something to try. But it was *life and death* for me. I *had* to sell. There was no way around it. *I had to sell a lot of accounts.*

This is how you collapse time: by being highly committed and putting systems in place to extract every last ounce of knowledge that could help you to perform more powerfully. I knocked relentlessly each day. Rejections, weather, mosquitoes, fatigue, or mental blocks couldn't stop me because I was committed to my wife and my sons—my holy cause.

Each day that summer, after returning to our apartments—sometimes as late as 10:00, 11:00, or midnight—I'd make five or six packages of ramen noodles and take them over to the apartments of the experienced reps. I ate and role-played with them until I fell asleep. I practiced overcoming every objection until I couldn't do it wrong. Amateurs practice until they get something right. Professionals practice until they can't do it wrong. And believe me, I practiced overcoming every type of objection as if my life depended on it, because it did. I committed to becoming a professional because I wanted to be paid like a professional.

In the mornings, if I wasn't practicing or listening, I'd invite other reps over to role-play over breakfast. I was on fire. I was committed. I was certain that if I could make up the time difference between the other experienced reps and me, I could make the money they were making. I committed to mastering these skills.

Most working days, I put in three to four extra hours of study and practice. Imagine that—three to four hours a day, five days a week, because on Saturday we knocked all day. I put in twenty bonus hours a week over twenty weeks—that's four hundred hours of bonus time that I had over the other rookies of the year, because I was committed to making this happen. In addition, on Sundays, while guys went swimming, golfing, or to the movies, I went to church, came home, and studied and practiced. I slept, ate, and then practiced some more. The window of opportunity was opening, and I chose to exploit it and break it wide open.

Knocking in neighborhoods late at night didn't mean I was knocking on doors and waking people up. I looked for the shift workers, the doors that never had anyone home during the day and garage lights on with the garage door open. Sometimes I'd get into the homes at 10:00 or 11:00 at night. Getting into homes late has nothing to do with luck; it has everything to do with skill. And high-level skills are developed through commitment.

Monday through Friday, we started at 2:00 p.m. Many days, I'd start as early as 9:00 a.m. I wanted the universe to know that I was going to outwork everybody in the office and in the company. I lived on a steady diet of energy drinks and potato chips. If someone had drawn blood from me that summer, I'm sure it would have smelled of Red Bull. I did what was required of me. I knocked early morning, late night, all day long. I never took time off because of frustration or fatigue, as many do.

I remember one day, as I was puking on the side of the road, my car leader said, "You've gotta go and rest."

I looked at him and said, "Only death can keep me off the doors today, man."

I drank two Red Bulls, ate a bag of chips, and got to the doors. You could have rightfully tattooed *100% Committed* on me that summer. Nothing could have stopped me.

Halfway through the summer, we made the move to Georgia from South Carolina, as we had planned to do. Before the official move, on Mondays, we would drive two and a half hours to Georgia, stay in hotels Monday and Tuesday night, and drive back late on Wednesday night, getting back around 1:00 a.m. We'd stock up and go back to Georgia on Thursday morning and stay until the end of day on Saturday, when we'd drive back to South Carolina. I will never forget those times. We were earning our money.

Competition Drives Performance

Working the doors was like playing football all over again. We had teams and competition. There had to be a complete "buy-in" of culture, "buy-in" of product, and "buy-in" of value for success. How bought in are you to your company, your business, your family, and your life? Without 100 percent buy-in, you're in trouble and you won't make it. You simply won't make it. It's easier to buy in when you have phenomenal leaders who lead with massive vision, and C-Baugh had vision.

My manager, Brandon Holmes (B-Holmes), also had vision, and he was instrumental in my success. I couldn't have asked for a better leader that summer. My wife and I had actually chosen another one of C-Baugh's managers early in the recruiting process, but then, the following morning, something inside me told me to talk with B-Holmes one more time. We chose his team, and that choice changed the entire course of my knocking career.

Eli Robertson was also responsible for helping me that first summer. He was the other top rookie on our team. He pushed me to sell early and late. Because he was naturally good at selling, I had to start earlier and work later to keep pace with him. We became great friends, and we're still close today.

I hustled and stayed relentless, like the Terminator. A lot of inefficiency in a job like sales can be made up with pure hustle. Like a basketball player who scraps for every loose ball, or the walk-on football player in college who doesn't know how to stop, hustle levels the playing field. I learned a lot that summer because I stayed open and humble, and then I would apply what I'd learned. You can teach skills, but you can't teach hard work. You can teach a salesman how to overcome objections, but you can't teach hustle. You have to learn how to be committed in your life every single day, and be clear about what you're committed to doing. I was committed that summer. Nothing would stop me.

By the end of the summer, I ended up being one of the top rookies in the company. I wasn't number one, as there were other rookies who had spent four months previously knocking on doors to make preseason sales. They had a huge advantage, and I just wasn't able to catch them. For the summer, I was in the top 1 percent for first-year reps.

Halfway through the summer I recruited a team from another company. On that team was a third-year rep by the name of Melvin White, who had mad skills in the game and showed me different strategies for the types of neighborhoods he knocked. Melvin could throw in five, six, or seven deals in the space of a few hours. Sometimes we think there's only one way to do a job, but in reality, there's always more than one way. Melvin came from a different tradition of door-to-door sales, and he gave me more tools to keep in my tool belt.

No one worked harder than I did that summer. When you want something bad enough that you're willing to sacrifice comfort, ego, and anything else to get it, you'll make it happen. I extended my time that summer by three weeks. While football season was going on, I was knocking every day. Of course, I questioned myself. Why in the world was I knocking on doors in the fall on Saturday afternoons? The answer was simple: because my goals were so big that summer that I was willing to sacrifice comfort to achieve my desired outcomes.

I'll never forget a day that July while I was in Georgia. My wife called in tears and said, "Thank you for providing for us, it's so nice to be able to go to the store again without having to worry about not having money or what I can or can't buy." I cried that day. I still get emotional when I think about the sacrifices, the grind and hustle we put into that first summer in South Carolina and Georgia.

I also loved the people in the South. Sure, I was selling them something that would be beneficial to them, but I really appreciated these people trusting me and letting me into their homes, and allowing me to provide value for them. I knocked in scary parts of town. I knocked in low-income neighborhoods, high-income neighborhoods, the backwoods, and any place that had a homeowner. I'm sure the prayers of my wife and sons brought angels down to protect me, as I had absolutely no fear in any area that I knocked. A couple of times that August I was so exhausted that I fell asleep on a prospective customer's couch while selling and woke up twenty minutes later. They said, "You fell asleep, but it's OK. If you need to rest, rest." Each time this happened, I sold the customer.

In looking at that pivotal summer, I go back to that first week in South Carolina, gazing into the sky and asking silently, *God, is this really it?* There was no answer, and so I made up my mind that if this was it, I was going to be the best and have the best attitude about it. I learned what it meant to be committed. Knocking doors is not for the faint of heart. You have to deal with rejection and uncomfortable weather, and it's a daily grind in which you only eat if you sell. The three-week extension period after the full summer of knocking revealed my deep commitment. Many guys couldn't do it. I had to do it. It was a must to succeed and leave a champion. It was a tough job, but C-Baugh was right—it was gratifying, fun, and challenging.

I had never felt so satisfied and grateful as I did finishing up the 2011 knocking season. I felt like I had when I finished up my two-year mission and my time playing football. I had given it my all. I did what was required. I was committed to the end. As we drove away from

Georgia, my heart swelled with pride and gratitude. I left it all out on the doors.

Questions to Consider Carefully and Answer:

- How committed are you to what you truly desire for your life?
- What would "collapsing time" look like for you in your business, your family, and your life?
- What would it take for you to wake up and start living your most productive and prosperous life?
- Are you still playing small in your life? If so, what is one thing you can do change that today?

CHAPTER 12

Rebuilding on Sweat Equity
Commitment Alters Everything

| I I I I I | I I I I I | I I I I I | I I I I I | I I I I I | I I I I I | I I I I

"Without hustle, talent will only carry you so far."
—Gary Vaynerchuk

H ow often do we think about or discuss things that we truly *want* in life?

"I *want* to lose weight."

"I *want* a more dynamic and electric marriage."

"I *want* to make more money."

"I *want* to be at the top of my company."

"I *want* to get better grades."

"I *want* a nicer home with a newer car, and for sure, I *want* more time to do what I really want to do."

"I *want* to coach Division I sports."

Or, maybe you've found yourself sick with the *need* bug.

"I *need* to hit the gym and lose fifty pounds."

"I *need* to be more patient with my children."

"I *need* to stop smoking."

"I *need* to quit procrastinating."

"I *need* to clean out the garage."

"I *need* to change my life."

If you've found yourself with the *want* or *need* bug, you're in deep trouble, and here's why: The majority of people who sit around and say "I want" or "I need" rarely seem to obtain their life's desires. How do I know this with certainty? Because at one time, *I was one of those people*.

Almost all of us *want* to make more money, lose more weight, have a better relationship with our loved ones, make a difference in the lives of others, travel the world, and feel like we really *lived*. Almost all of us *need* to do something that we have put off for some time. So what separates the people who sit around and discuss their wants and needs from those who actually achieve their intended results? What's the difference between those still waiting, wanting, wishing, hoping, needing, and those who have already been there, done that, and are still doing it?

There's certainly no shortage of information available to you on how to change your life, acquire more clients, find more peace, make more money, lose weight, or start that business. There's no shortage of information on how to grow your company, raise your children more effectively, recruit more powerful players to your team, or become number one in your industry. It's not a lack of knowledge that holds you back. So what is it?

What is it that allows you to gain and accomplish your desires and everything you truly want out of life?

It is **COMMITMENT**.

Commitment means you get the job done, no matter what. You don't make excuses, even if there *are* excuses for not getting the results you desire. When you're committed, there's no going back. You commit to achieving your target, regardless of the challenge. You find a way to hit your target, regardless of the seen and unforeseen obstacles. The story about Cortés and his men from chapter 11 is a perfect illustration of commitment.

I burned my ships when I entered the door-to-door industry in 2011. I was committed. I quit blogging, I stopped marketing, and I ended every other business venture in which I was involved. I knew my *why* for knocking on doors. Commitment means that you're willing to sacrifice the comfortable, easy, wide path along which most people stroll leisurely in life. Are you willing to do whatever it takes for your *why*, for your holy cause? When you commit, the necessary required actions become a quest rather than a burden.

The word *commitment* has been overused in reference to personal growth and development. Because of their casual use, the meaning of *commit, committed,* and *commitment* appear weak and without authority. If you are serious about transforming any part of your life, you cannot afford to take a casual or part-time approach in this endeavor.

Commitment Alters Everything

Transformation is real. Any man or woman who undergoes real transformation only does so with strong, continual commitment over time. That means he or she doesn't commit once, but rather, every single day.

Commitment a year ago may not bring about the necessary required actions to produce results today. This is why a daily renewal of one's agreements and deep commitments is necessary.

One way to ignite that deep commitment is to live in game mode—competition with yourself or others—or "crisis" mode, whether the crisis is real or invented. All excuses and obstacles evaporate when you bring commitment to your handling of a competition or crisis. Are you truly committed to your desired reality?

When I speak with clients about commitment, if they bring up an excuse about not having enough time or not having enough money, I simply tell them they are not committed. Being uncommitted is NOT a bad thing either.

When the uncommitted have a difficult time seeing this, I ask, "If your child or spouse were drowning in a river, would you *try* to save him or her or would you actually do so?"

Their response 100 percent of the time, is, without hesitation, "I would save [him/her]."

"Would you give it your best shot or would you save him or her?" I ask again.

Again their response is, "I would save [him/her]."

Commitment works the same way. Once you dedicate yourself to a deep holy cause or higher purpose (saving your loved ones, living your higher calling in life, serving others for a greater cause, generating life-changing income), you become committed, and committing daily becomes who you are. Without clarity on what you want and a holy cause behind that clarity, there's no need for a significant commitment.

When you commit fully, the results inevitably appear. I was in crisis mode in 2011. I played to win. Scratch that; forget about winning. I played to own and dominate the game.

The one thing that alters everything is commitment. Once you're committed, everything begins to show up for you in your life. Big reasons and excuses that once seemed to stand as mountains blocking your way become tiny pebbles in the path of your ruthless commitment.

To the uncommitted person, a lack of resources means he or she can't pursue his or her goals. A lack of resources means nothing to one who is committed. The highly committed individual creates options almost out of thin air. As Tony Robbins says, "It's not about resources; it's about being resourceful." And being resourceful comes from being highly committed. How committed are you to your life, your spouse, your children, and your career? How committed are you to results?

Aron Ralston is another great example of commitment. When you commit, you will be required to sacrifice. In his book, *Between a Rock and a Hard Place,* Ralston tells the story of how he was trapped by a boulder for more than five days after a hiking mishap in southeastern Utah. How do we know he was committed to living? Because he cut off his own arm with a dull multi-tool, rappelled sixty feet down, hiked five miles out, and lived to tell the story.

I've never cut off my arm, so I can only imagine having to decide between cutting off my arm and staying put, hoping that maybe someone will find me. What would cause an individual to sacrifice his arm? Ralston sacrificed because he was committed to his loved ones and to his life. Let me say that again. *He was committed to his loved ones and to his life.* He had a holy cause.

Are you willing to cut off things, like Aron Ralston did, to get to the next level in your life? C-Baugh would often say, "You've gotta *give up* to *go up.*"

To be committed means there is no other path to take but the narrow one that leads you above and beyond your comfort zone. It's anything but easy, but it's worth it. Will you be uncomfortable at times? Yes. Being highly committed means you get comfortable being uncomfortable. If you don't ever step out of that comfort zone, you will miss the greatest moments in your life because you allowed excuses to stop you from playing big.

If commitment becomes casual, our priorities rearrange, our dreams shrink, and the big goals that were once within reach elude us like a thief in the night. Don't let your commitment become casual. Casual fighters end up dying because they train casually. The same goes for casual commitment. Casually committed people don't produce results because there's no such thing as casual commitment. You're either in or out. There's no in between with commitment.

One of the greatest gifts that came as a result of my having lost everything between 2007 and 2011 was learning not only to understand commitment, but also to live it. I had to be committed in order to extract myself from my current situation and reinvent my life.

Sincere Commitments Create Results

Commitment can be summed up in this simple three-step definition:

1. Doing what is required to create your intended result
2. Doing what you said you would do to create your intended result
3. Acting decisively in spite of thoughts, feelings, emotions, and moods to create your intended result

Did you do what is required to create the intended result, or did you do something else? Doing what is required brings results. Doing something else ... well, that gets you something else. I did what was required that first summer of knocking. I didn't just do my best. I didn't do what I knew; I did what was required.

Are you a person who does what he says he will do? One of my coaches taught me that if all we did were honor our word, we would achieve powerful results. Living without integrity creates stress and misery. It's also unworkable.

Can you act in spite of thoughts, feelings, emotions and moods? I can hear it now: "I don't feel like exercising," or "I don't feel like talking to people about my business," or "I'm not in the mood to learn new skills." Powerful people act decisively. Non-powerful people are governed by how they feel at the time, or by the mood they are in. Non-powerful people allow doubtful thoughts to run rampant. Powerful people just do what's required regardless of the thoughts they have in their minds. Non-powerful people only act when they feel like it. Powerful people embrace imperfect action regardless of whether they feel like it or not. Mood is irrelevant when you're highly committed.

You never simply receive what you "need" or what you desire. You get what you commit to. How do you know what your current commitments are? Just look at your life. Look at your results. Look at your bank account. Look at your marriage. Look at the scale. Look at your spirituality. Look at what you have and who you are.

Jesus said, "By their fruits ye shall know them." Your "fruits" are your results. If you're unhappy with any aspect of your life, clarify what you want and then make a real commitment to creating it. What commitment would you have to make today to make real changes in your life?

Commitment "moves" you—literally. It changes you physiologically and rewires how you see yourself and how you see the world, thereby producing new actions that bring about entirely new results.

Dusan Djukich sums it up perfectly in his masterpiece, *Straight-Line Leadership*:

When I am unclear about my commitment, I procrastinate. When I am clear about my commitment, I act. When I am unclear about my commitment, I talk about my job. When I am clear about my commitment, I do my job. When I am unclear about my commitment, I maintain my image. When I am clear about my commitment, I maintain my integrity. When I am unclear about my commitment, I play it safe. When I am clear about my commitment, I empower others.

Commitment is underrated. But guess what? Commitment is the new currency. Give me a person who is highly committed, and I will give you a person who can create the "impossible" at will.

Questions to Consider Carefully and Answer:

- What purpose or mission in your life would bring about a deep commitment?
- Name a time in the past when you were highly committed. What results did you produce with that commitment?
- What are you looking to create or resolve in your life that would require a meaningful commitment?
- What are you unhappily settling for that could be improved by making a deep commitment?
- What does it mean to be committed?
- What new commitments must you make today to create the future you yearn to have?

CHAPTER 13

When It's Time to Walk Away, Do It
The Faith to Leap

|ııııı|ııııı|ııııı|ııııı|ııııı|ııııı|ııııı

> *"Almost every successful person begins with*
> *two beliefs: The future can be better than the*
> *present, and I have the power to make it so."*
> —David Brooks

In 2011, I returned home, triumphant from my first summer of knocking. My wife and I found a place in Orem, Utah, and I felt like God had delivered a gift to us. It was beautiful. I was once again reminded that God can be involved in the intimate details of our lives as much as we allow Him to be.

In November of 2011, I went out on a preseason trip, selling, recruiting, and staying sharp. I trusted C-Baugh and did the required work to become great in the industry as I continued to provide for my family. These trips provided stark contrasts for me: There was the abundance and joy of family life at home in Utah, and then there was the loneliness and isolation of the trips. When I was away, there was nothing to do except study, sell, and work out. I hated being away from my wife and sons. I still do. Sure, I had made great money and gained wonderful friends in the company, but I was still looking for something else. In my heart, I felt I was meant to do something different. I prayed and sought God's help often.

I began recruiting a team and going on more preseason trips. In the beginning of 2012, I went to Texas for two weeks. Once again, I was away from my family, but it was to master my skills, train, and get sales. I continued to pay the piper and it worked.

That first summer on the doors was in South Carolina and Georgia. The second summer of knocking was in the great state of Texas. I'd spent my first summer learning how to sell, in order to make money for my wife and kids and get out of the rut we were in from the mortgage and real estate collapse.

The second summer, I was a car driver, manager, and leader from the front. I recruited and recruited. I teamed up with a couple of other managers who were bosses in the industry, and we took on the Austin, Texas, market. I coached my team to perform at higher levels.

In that second summer, I realized I needed to dig deeper for what I wanted to do. Earlier that year something had told me, *Hey, maybe your path is to go get a master's degree.* I put some thought and prayer into it and began to feel good about the hunch. I talked to my wife and we both felt optimistic about it. The reality was that I didn't want to knock doors anymore. I still felt I was meant to do something else with my life, so doing a master's program made sense.

I applied to BYU and was accepted, which meant I needed to make money again so I could pay for school. And that brought me back to knocking and into Texas. After that summer, however, it was time to start the program. I went into it with an open and enthusiastic heart, but before long, I realized it was another detour, rather than the answer. Now what?

Choosing the Right Path

There is a story of a man and his son who went out sightseeing in the Grand Canyon area on the Utah-Arizona border. On their way home, they came to an unfamiliar fork in the road. They said a prayer and asked, "Which road should we take?" They both felt they should take the right road at the fork, so they did. Five minutes down the road, they came to an abrupt dead end, which made them realize they needed to take the other road.

The young boy asked his father, "Why do you think that happened?"

His father replied, "Sometimes God allows us to go down a path so that we know for certain it's not for us."

This was the master's program for me. I knew that the public sector was not my arena, but I only knew it because I'd spent a full semester at school. I'm an entrepreneur. I'd been an entrepreneur since coming home from the NFL, and that was my path. Now I knew for certain that I could put all my time, energy, and money into my business.

When I left BYU at the end of 2012, I knew I would never go back. I left my locker filled with books, protein powder, and whatever else I had in there. I was done with school. I am grateful that BYU allowed me to return so I could know with surety what my next step would be. When I'd started that fall, I'd had visions of graduating, finishing strong, and doing something other than knocking doors. Yet the familiar thing we often run from sometimes becomes the greatest path to power and victory for us. Like Jonah in the Old Testament, sometimes the very thing we run from is the very thing that would deliver us.

That meant that for a third summer, I would knock on doors and lead my men to their personal victories. In my third summer of knocking, I recruited Eli back to Vivint. He was the other top first-year rep from our first summer in South Carolina. He was running an entire company in Hawaii during 2012.

We knew that the secret to having a big summer was having big preseason trips and getting guys through the early learning curve of knocking and selling. Preseason also separated the committed from the interested. It's a best practice to weed out of your systems earlier rather than later people who show less commitment.

Preseason for knocking on doors is September till mid-April, while summer season is mid-April until the end of August. We took our team on a preseason trip to Texas for two weeks in January 2013. We drove twenty-four hours straight, slept a few hours, and then began the daily work of protecting families and protecting neighborhoods.

We had a singular focus: to be the top first-year team. After arriving home from this two-week trip in January, we embarked on another two-week trip in February. Then we took a ten-day trip in March. We were gone for nearly six weeks between January and the end of March. It was the price we had to pay. So often, we want big results, big money, great relationships, and a life of real comfort, but the majority of people aren't willing to pay the price to get it. We were paying the piper that year. We were committed, and the fruits of our labor would be plentiful in the fall. Preseason had wrapped up and it was go time. And sure enough, we were the top first-year team that preseason.

Get the First One under Your Belt

I drove to Iowa early in April to set up shop with a couple of other guys that I had recruited. No matter how many times you've done something, the process of it can still jolt you into a brutal reality. I could say as much about my time in Iowa. It was so cold right off the bat that I wanted to quit, but, of course, quitting is never an option when you're committed to a holy cause.

"Feeling" like quitting was a sign that I was stepping onto the sacred grounds of growth and expansion. Iowa wasn't what I thought it would be. Iowa wasn't Georgia or Texas. Iowa was in the bone-chilling

Midwest, with weather that would make many of the men question their resolve. The reality of management is that you have to get that first real year under your belt. I needed this first year of "really managing" on my own. My first summer was pure selling and producing while learning from B-Holmes. My second summer, I was a co-manager with two other seasoned managers, Eliason and Schreiner, who were absolute beasts in the industry. The difficulties I faced in Iowa in 2013 were personal growing pains.

In every part of life, there is always that big and scary "first time" that you can't avoid. There's the first time you go on a date, get a job, play sports, or present on a stage. There's the first book, the first speech, the first high-end client, and the first time being a CEO. There's a first time for everything, and you must be willing to face it. No one can save you from this "first time." For me, this was the first time opening up shop at the beginning of summer, and it was real. No one could save me. No one could do it for me. It was something I needed to go through.

I had to deal with apartments, city licensing, motivating my guys, and knocking in the brisk Midwest weather. This was challenging for me. I remember reaching out to my wife and saying, "I can't believe I'm doing this again. I can't believe I'm here again." It was like when you prepare all off-season for the football season, and then football camp starts and it's harder and more difficult than you expected. Suddenly, you look at your teammates and ask, "Am I really doing this again?"

Being a head football coach in college looks like fun. Being a top-producing sales regional looks glamorous. Being a Hollywood blockbuster star looks exciting. Being a social media celebrity seems like it would be all fun and no work. Being a top CEO looks like it's all vacations and high-end living.

The reality? They all have their icy-cold days, as I was having in Iowa.

The work done behind the scenes is not pretty. In fact, it can be so stressful that it can crush the average human being. But I'm not average, and I'm not even satisfied with being *good*. And honestly, you aren't average either. You were born to be great and to do something incredible with your life. For me, I want to be the best. Still, Iowa was difficult.

The not-so-pretty part of the job is what separates the few from the rest. Seth Godin calls it "being in the dip," and I was deep in the dip. It's true that what doesn't kill you only makes you stronger. It's also true that while pressure can burst pipes, it can also produce diamonds. This is what the beginning of April in Iowa was doing for me. What so many don't understand is that success is not sexy. Greatness requires arduous, boring work that doesn't look like what we see on TV or in magazines. You don't see the "cold Iowa mornings" every superstar, professional athlete, Hollywood actor, C-level executive, and high-level sales manager endures.

The price of success is high, but it's also payable by anyone committed to paying it. You'll have moments that make you question, and when they come, embrace them, step into them, and know that "this too shall pass" if you remain focused and dedicated and keep moving forward. As one of my coaches so often told me, "Invite and embrace the pain."

The cure-all in any sales job is sales. Not a single one of the guys was selling when we opened up Iowa, and I wasn't either. I felt like we were losing guys early on, and we did. C-Baugh rallied the troops and sent Dan Tracy, the regional sales trainer who'd showed me my first sale in Idaho in 2011. Dan showed up and spent a week helping me to get things rolling during that difficult time.

You need good people in your life to help you. No matter how great you are, no matter how skilled you are, you'll need that outside perspective from someone else to guide you. Perspective always creates possibilities. I reached out to another mentor and brother,

Garrett J. White, with whom I'd had many powerful conversations over the years. He coached me through this difficult but necessary time early in April.

When it was all said and done, I loved my time in Iowa. Why? Because I persisted and stayed committed. No one ever said, "I'm happy I gave less than my best." By the time I finished, I could sell to any home in any neighborhood—small homes, big homes, old homes, and new homes. Young couples, old couples, widows, military members, CEOs, doctors, engineers, and single parents. Asians, Polynesians, African-Americans, Indians, Caucasians—it didn't matter who or where they were from. If they had a desire to listen to the offer and it made sense, we were able to protect their home.

We covered the entire state of Iowa from Davenport on the east side to Cedar Rapids, Waterloo, and Iowa City in the middle, all the way west to Des Moines. This was my third summer, and I'd had a big year. In fact, I had doubled my income every year I had done the job.

On the last knocking day of 2013, I got home at about 10:00 p.m., packed up the apartment, and drove straight to Utah. I pulled over a few times to sleep for an hour or two, but the satisfaction of finishing the summer strong powered the long drive home (along with a few 5-Hour Energy shots).

When I finally arrived home, our regional manager immediately held a retreat with all the managers. I accepted the fact that this was it. I hadn't wanted to knock my first summer, but I'd gone out for the holy cause. My reason for knocking the second summer had been to fund my master's program. By the time my third summer had rolled around, I was 100 percent invested. When you want something bad enough, and the *why* is deep enough, and you're 100 percent committed, the required work becomes irrelevant, regardless of how difficult it may be. The grind of knocking on doors became irrelevant. My job became simple: Wake up, prep, do the work, express gratitude, go to sleep, and then repeat.

At this point, I'd accepted that this was my career path. I committed to make a five-year run, which meant two more years doing what we were doing, and then my wife and I could reevaluate.

I began mapping out the next few years to figure out how I was going to climb to the top to become a regional manager. C-Baugh always said the doors needed to be a three-to-five year run to make it worth it, because it wasn't until at least the third year that you had enough of the real skills locked and loaded to produce that big influx of life-changing income. He was right, but I was unprepared for what would happen during that postseason period.

Listening to the Voice

A month after making the commitment to go long-term and climb to the top, I was in Bakersfield, California, on another preseason trip. The same voice that had said, "Go and knock" in 2011, and that had later said, "Go to school," was now telling me that it was time to move on. Crazy, right? Just as I was enjoying the job and envisioning what could be, I heard and felt the voice. I couldn't believe what I was feeling! How could this be? I was making great money. I had fantastic friends and relationships. I loved the leadership and culture of the company. I had come to enjoy knocking and going on trips. But at the same time, I couldn't ignore the feeling that I was meant to fulfill what had long been my dream: to coach, speak, and inspire. I had achieved so much on the doors. I had proven that I could do whatever I set my mind to do.

When I told my wife it was time to leave Vivint, she cried. It was difficult for me to tell her. She didn't want me to leave Vivint, a place that had been so good to us. I had tried to coach and consult in the past, immediately after the mortgage meltdown. I'd failed miserably because I had lacked the mind-set and skill set to do it properly. I didn't know what I was doing back then, nor did I have the coaches and mentors I needed to help me succeed. My wife had sat by and watched me fail.

She was such a supporter and had suffered along with me as we sold everything we had in the run between 2007 and 2011.

I knew that between October 2013 and January 2014, I had a decision to make. Do I ignore the voice and continue with the job to follow the money? Do I do both—coach and work with Vivint? Or do I walk away from the success and listen to the voice telling me to go coach? I wanted, as Stephen Covey put it, to "unleash human potential." I was committed to leading people to live their greatest versions of themselves, what I call the *Prosperity Revolution*. The voice moved me and spoke to me: *You're done. It's time to leap.*

It's challenging when the voice speaks to you. You've got to listen. You have to trust that when you follow it, the way will be prepared and things will work in your favor. It doesn't mean it will be easy. It means you have to have trust that, ultimately, the way will open up before you, even if it opens up at the last moment.

I told my business partner Eli first, and he understood. I then sat with the man who had recruited me: my mentor and brother, C-Baugh. It was difficult; C-Baugh had delivered on everything he'd promised during our conversation at the Happy Sumo back in 2011. He'd watched me reach my goals, and then soar beyond. But I believe he knew it was coming.

I wasn't the first to walk away from the industry. Other top guys had left to become sports agents, business owners, and other significant leaders of industries. I walked away, and I walked away on top.

If you're going to get to that next level in your life, you have to learn to let go. You have to recognize when it's time to walk ... or leap. And when you do listen, let go, and make that leap, you'll experience quantum growth that most people never experience.

My time recruiting and knocking on doors was done, and those three summers on the doors had changed my life. It was a refiner's fire. It forged me and prepared me for the next step. My confidence was at an all-time high, and our bank accounts were proof of that. Once again, I listened to the voice, and this time, it told me it was time to leave. So I left.

Will you listen to the voice inside you? Do you have courage to do the difficult things you are called to do?

Part of rebuilding and re-engineering your life may involve taking that job that you don't want to do. Drop your ego, swallow your pride, and embrace whatever you need to do. It may only be for a season, or it may be for the rest of your life. If you do it right, it will launch you toward your greatest destiny.

Questions to Consider Carefully and Answer:

- To whom can you reach out for perspective when you need help?
- Are you a serial quitter, or can you finish what you start?
- Do you know and recognize that voice, that feeling that guides you?
- If you're currently in a financial bind, are you willing to take on a job to get certainty back, or does your ego prevent you from doing it?
- If you're in a great position financially, can you hear what the voice is telling you to do?
- Will you listen even when the voice makes no sense?

CHAPTER 14

Lessons in Leading
To Lead, First Be Led

*"Once you've found your own voice, the choice to
expand your influence, to increase your contribution,
is the choice to inspire others to find their voice."*
—Stephen Covey

Setema, can you please call me? It was a text message from a plastic surgeon I had met earlier that year, in 2014. She had called me a few times in a row.

"Take care of the boys," I told my wife. "I'll be right back."

It was a beautiful Saturday morning, and I stepped outside while my boys were getting haircuts. I called the surgeon, a mother of two children. She talked. I listened. I listened more and then I opened up to her. I shared with her what she needed to hear in order to empower her life. I began to coach her.

Coaching people is not about giving clever advice or warm, fuzzy suggestions. Real coaching is for highly committed people who want real results. Real coaching is listening intently and being present, and then getting them to see what they cannot see. I always wanted to coach, teach, and speak from stage—to lead men and women to their greatest lives possible. And now it was happening in real time.

We spent an hour on the phone together that day, and I followed up with her a couple of days later.

After our second conversation she asked, "What do I need to do to continue working with you?" I told her what it would take: a real commitment and a significant investment in herself. She was in. We started a week later. In the time that we worked together, so much changed in her life.

This was the beginning of a furious seven-month run of coaching, leveling up, webinar trainings, sales trainings, helping others to get results, and showing my wife I could produce outside of the two-billion dollar company called Vivint.

It wasn't always this good. In October of 2013, when I decided it was time to walk away from Vivint, my wife didn't want me to do it because I had failed miserably years earlier. I felt like Bill Belichick, the head coach of the Cleveland Browns in the early 1990s. He failed miserably in Cleveland, and he was practically run out of town. Then he came back to serve as an assistant coach to Bill Parcells in New England, and again, with the New York Jets. He was hired as head coach of the New England Patriots in 2000, and has since gone on to win four Super Bowls by the time of this writing. I am confident he will get one or two more before he wraps up his career.

Yes, failure is part of the game. Failure is the sure path to success. If you're not failing, you're not pushing hard enough. When you fail, you step back, recalibrate, and step up again. I stepped up again and was ready for round two of fulfilling my dream.

Permission Granted

Everything began to change when I flew down to Laguna Beach to spend time with one of my coaches.

Garrett looked at me and said, "Why don't you just give yourself permission, Setema? Just give yourself permission. You were the top at BYU in football. You were a Super Bowl champ. You dominated the doors. You dominated the mortgage and real estate arena back in the day. You spent two years of your life learning a new language and teaching people in a third world country and were a leader there. You had success. Why do you continue to refuse to own it?"

Why didn't I give myself permission to be great? What was it inside me that insisted I keep playing small? It was as if I had never accessed full power, not even in football. But I wasn't going to let that happen anymore. I was going to give myself permission.

Yes, having a powerful coach works. That day Garrett gave me a gift that became the sparks that would ignite a fire deep within me.

I made a habit of attending workshops, symposiums, seminars, and masterminds. That kind of commitment is crucial if your purpose is to expand and create value for others. It is difficult to create value for others if you haven't become valuable to the marketplace, and value is always expressed through skills.

Two weeks after that conversation with Garrett, I flew back down and attended another event in Laguna Beach with my group of men who were working to maximize their potential and better their lives, my Warrior brothers. That weekend, I launched a coaching program. I had invested heavily in coaches, but didn't yet have the power and certainty to demand such an investment from other people consistently. So, I just started where I was and went from there. I began group coaching, and was able to increase my fees steadily as my clients grew in number. I knew I had a gift. In addition to group coaching, I began coaching clients one-on-one over the phone, and the results were awesome to see.

I was beginning to put in long days, from 7:00 in the morning until about 6:00 or 7:00 at night. Sometimes I spoke with people at midnight because that was the best time to coach them. I was on the phone all day coaching. I was conducting webinars and Skype calls. As I finished out 2014, the investments I'd made a year earlier were starting to pay off in a big way.

I've been asked, "Why did you hire three coaches?"

My answer: Because I felt it was necessary at the time.

I hired Garrett in late 2013. I attended mastermind groups led by Kevin Nations on two different occasions in January and in February. And I hired a third coach by the name of Scott Byrd, who was completely different from Garrett and Kevin. All three men helped me tremendously. To this day, I still utilize what I learned from each. I grew tremendously by having Garrett at my side teaching me, leading me, and helping me to see things. Garrett made it possible for me to move out of Utah to Southern California. He helped me access a power within that had gone untapped for most of my life. He helped me to truly "level up" every part of my life.

It can be scary to invest in yourself and get the mentoring and coaching you need, but if you do the work and work with the right coach, the returns can be as much as 1,000 percent. I'll always have a coach in my life. Even as I write this book I have a couple of coaches in whom I have invested. You are reading this book because I paid a coach to help me finish it.

It's too costly to go without perspective and insight. It's also hypocritical as a coach and consultant to want people to pay me if I am not paying someone else. I see this in the coaching world too often: coaches and consultants who want people to pay them big money, but who are, themselves, unwilling to pay big money to be coached. It doesn't work that way. This is one reason why most coaches never make it.

In order to change your life, you are going to have to be able to lead yourself first. Before you can be a leader for others, the first person you are going to have to lead is yourself. Can you lead yourself? Can you give yourself permission to be great? Can you do the work when you are alone and no one is watching?

By the end of 2014, I had found my groove as a coach. I was coaching everyone from network marketers, trainers, and coaches to business owners, realtors, and real estate investors. I coached surgeons, athletes, fitness entrepreneurs, and sales managers. I had public speakers and owners of construction companies in my group. It was amazing.

Garrett became a guiding light for me as I traversed this new business terrain of coaching and consulting. He helped me see some things I would never have noticed without him. Time with Garrett was invaluable; he was a key figure for me early in my coaching days, just as C-Baugh had been for me in my Vivint days.

I've had spiritual mentors, business coaches, nutrition coaches, and everything in between. At the end of the day, a coach will help you see what you can't see. A coach will point out the flaws that you refuse to confront, and a coach will punch you in the face—figuratively speaking (but sometimes literally, if necessary).

It makes sense to have a coach if you desire to expand, improve, and do better for yourself. Athletes have coaches. Actors have coaches. C-level executives have coaches and advisors. Eight-figure earners have coaches. If you've never had a real coach to guide you, you're missing out.

You really don't need much to scoot along in life and play it safe. But if you want to take things to another level, having someone in your corner gives you the edge you need to collapse time and become who you were meant to become.

As a coach, I am often led to people, and people are led to me. I coach people in their marriages and show them how to revitalize relationships that have gone stale. I coach people in their businesses and help them solve problems that otherwise would have been extremely costly. I coach parents with their children and help them to become clear about what they truly want and implement the necessary required actions to accomplish those desires. I work with highly committed people on all types of personal issues that prevent them from leveling up in life.

I coach people on every conversation, from prayer to marketing to sales to bedtime rituals for their children. I help them confront things they've been avoiding for years. I help my clients become juggernauts, or as Dusan Djukich says, "a powerful, unstoppable group of people dedicated to an agreed-upon purpose."

I've sometimes yelled so loudly at my clients that my boys have come running to my door, asking, "Are you OK, Daddy?" Coaching high performers is not some theoretical feel-good activity. It requires real tenacity, deep courage, and intense grit. From crucial conversations about dating for single entrepreneurs to critical high-profit environments where multimillion-dollar deals are on the line, I grow through my clients and my clients grow through me. While I help them, they help me. It's a true win-win—the only way to do business.

I still receive messages from that surgeon with two children. She reports that her children are happy, she is very content as a working mother, and her marriage is better than ever. From the men I've coached, I often receive messages that read, *I love and miss you, brother* or *Our work together helped me to solve some major issues within my company today.* I have come to view these types of relationships as the most important a human being can have. Being with another person in a space of honesty and trust is the most powerful thing I have ever experienced. I love what I do, and I love the people whom I serve.

I help people solve the hidden problems that hold them back from being the greatest versions of themselves and from living their highest purpose. In business, I help solve the most expensive problems and help individuals get through the challenges they face. I help my clients to produce RESULTS.

If my message resonates with you in your heart and soul, and if you would like to have a conversation, simply reach out through my site www.SetemaGali.com and let's talk. I love helping highly committed people create new possibilities and commit to the "impossible."

What's the difference between me and a coach who teaches people skills, such as marketing or writing headlines? Simply put, I work with people on who they are *being* rather than on the *how-tos*. How-tos are a different game. Just Google any subject, and you'll obtain the information you want and need. Knowing how to *be*? That's a different story.

I will coach, speak, and train for the rest of my life. Next to being a five-star husband and five-star daddy, this is my work and my calling. I love it.

Do you love what you do? Does it provide you the resources to contribute and grow in the way that you desire? If not, you have two choices:

1. Learn how to love it.
2. Retire and find something you love that you can be the best at, and that can pay you what you desire.

When I stood in front of my bankruptcy attorney in 2010, I knew I would eventually get to where I am today—and yet, where I am today is a thousand times better than I could have imagined. Don't settle. You can win no matter where you are or who you've been. I am living proof of it.

Questions to Consider Carefully and Answer:

- How would your life be different if you had a high-performance, powerful coach to help you confront what you've been avoiding?
- What is it costing you right now to stay stuck where you are?
- When was the last time you got outside yourself, gained perspective, and then applied it immediately? What were the results?
- What difference would a coach, consultant, or mentor make in your business, your marriage, and your health—if you were highly committed to following through?

CHAPTER 15

The Golden Thread
Learning to Love the Voice

| | | | | | | | | | | | | | | | | | | | | | | | | | | | | | | | | | | |

"The 'still, small voice' of God never calls on me to be like
another man. It appeals to me to rise to my full stature
and fulfill the promise that sleeps within my being."
—Sam Keen

A s I took the car seat out of my wife's car to put it in my truck, I heard that voice that had spoken to me many times before. This time, it was as clear as a voice that I would hear from my wife or any other person.

"Don't take your truck. Take your wife's car."

I didn't want to take my wife's car. I wanted to take my truck.

I took one more step, and the voice said again, "Don't take your truck. Take your wife's car."

I felt it, and knew this was important. I put the car seat down on the garage floor and stood there for five seconds, looking up to the sky. *God, is that you?*

I couldn't deny the voice. I put the car seat back in my wife's car.

When she came out, she said, "I thought we were taking your truck."

I told her, "No, I feel like we should take your car."

"OK," she said, and turned to the car. She's learned that when I say I "feel," we should do something; we should just do it. She knows it's more than a hunch.

Nothing happened that night in my wife's car, but a week later, as I was driving my truck for the first time since that voice had spoken to me, the brakes went out on the freeway while I was going seventy miles per hour. Fortunately, I was able to pump the brakes and downshift in order to get off I-15 and park the truck. Adrenaline shot through my body and my heart was filled with immense appreciation and gratitude. What would have happened had I not listened the week before? That week we had driven up into the mountains so that I could speak to a group. I could only imagine what it would have been like to come out of the mountains and have the brakes go out, trying to react quickly on a tiny mountain road through the canyons.

The voice always speaks and guides, but you have to be willing to listen to it, and more important, you must position yourself to hear and feel it.

In my life, I've learned to love the voice. It's the same voice that told me, "You need to go knock on doors." The same voice that said, "You should return to school for a master's degree," and then, "You're not doing this anymore." The same voice that said, "It's time to leap."

I cannot emphasize this enough: There are going to be scary times in your life when you're going to hear this voice and have a feeling, and it's not going to make any sense at all. But if you listen, the path will always open up and things will turn in your favor.

In 1998, I was a student at BYU and a teacher at the Missionary Training Center for the LDS Church. My scholarship check had run out, and I was starving that day. I was headed to BYU to go to class, and

I prayed to God, *I'm just so hungry. Please send me some food. Somehow, just send me something.*

As I parked my car down at the field house and walked up those big stairs that led to the campus, I turned right to go to class. Then the voice came to me. I suddenly felt that I should turn around and go into the Smith Family Living Center. I stopped and heard the voice again.

"Turn around and go into the Smith Family Living Center."

I turned around and walked into the building. I was wearing a dress shirt and tie because I was teaching that day at the M.T.C. Everyone in the building was also all dressed up. Behind the groups of well-dressed adults stood big tables of all-you-can-eat food: eggs, croissants, fruit, sausage, bagels, and orange juice. They motioned to me to get a plate, as if I were supposed to be there. My heart was filled with joy. As I walked out with my plate of food, I was so grateful. God had answered my prayers that day, as He had many times before, and as He will many times in the future.

Let the voice guide you, even when what it's telling you to do seems impossible. I remember one day in June of 2012, as I was knocking on doors, the voice told me to go to another neighborhood on my map. That wasn't part of my plan. I wanted to stay right where I was because to go to the other neighborhood meant I'd have to get in my car, drive there, and waste four to five minutes. So I stayed, but I kept picturing where I needed to go.

Finally, I said, "Lord, I trust you."

I got in my car and drove to the neighborhood. It was a five-minute drive. The first five doors were brutal.

"No, get the hell out of here."

"What are you doing here?"

"We don't need your kind here."

"Leave."

"Can you read the sign on the door? No soliciting."

At the fifth door, I thought, *OK, God, you told me to come here. What's going on?*

The sixth door I knocked on was the purpose. The homeowners invited me inside. I told them about the home automation and the security, safety, and preventative measures we took with these systems. The woman began to cry.

She said, "We wanted to get a security system, but one company turned us down, and my husband is getting ready to deploy to Afghanistan." She said it was an answer to her prayer. Indeed, it was.

I've had the voice speak to me in the smallest of ways, like helping me find my glasses. I lost them in the fall of 1994, when I was a freshman in college. Six months later, I sat in a religion class and the teacher talked about being humble in asking God, and that He would answer if we had faith and it was His will. The next morning, I knelt at my bedside in prayer. I prayed and asked God to help me find my glasses. I had complete faith that He would. Why were the glasses so important? I couldn't see very well without them and I didn't want to trouble my parents by asking them to buy me another pair. A picture of the Wilkinson Student Center popped into my mind. I went there, and they brought out a big bin of glasses. Mine weren't in there. Disappointed, I turned to walk out, and the voice told me to go back and tell them that I had lost my glasses six months earlier. When I told them that, they pulled out another bin, and my glasses were in it. That night, my prayers were pure gratitude for the guidance.

The voice will often come in thoughts or pictures, accompanied by a feeling that whatever you're seeing or hearing is right. When you listen to that voice, that divine guidance, you're led to experiences that appear miraculous. I can also tell you what happens when you don't listen to the voice.

I came home from my mission in the summer of 1997 and my brother told me, "Hey, I've got these two subwoofers. I was just going to give them away. We'll put them in your car."

Immediately a voice said, "Don't put them in your car. Don't do it."

You'd think that since I'd just come off a mission, I'd listen. But I didn't, and we put them in my car. A week later, someone broke into my car, shattered the windows, ripped out the speakers, tore out the stereo, and stole everything in my vehicle, including over a hundred CDs. That wouldn't have happened if I'd just listened to the still, small voice.

Listening to the voice in your life means you've got to be willing to obey, especially when it goes against what you want. One of my coaches once told me that if I were going to live the life that I wanted to live and do the things I felt called to do, I'd probably have to move out of Utah. Our environment shapes so much of what we see, what we do, and how we see ourselves; I grew up in Utah, and it's where my family is. Family is very important to me, my wife, and my sons, so it made no logical sense to move.

In January of 2015, I was part of the Wake Up Warrior team running Warrior Week with my brother Garrett White. I felt like it was truly time to take the next step for my life, my business, and my family. Garrett had been telling me for months that in order to create what I truly wanted to create, I would need to move out of Utah. It made no sense, but the voice spoke to me, and I knew this was a leap of faith that would take us to another level.

I called my wife and said, "Hey, we're moving to Arizona."

Two days later, I called her and told her, "Check that, we're moving to California." She thought I was joking until I posted on Facebook, *We're moving from Utah County to Orange County.*

In the beginning it was scary moving to Orange County. The prices of everything in SoCal are higher than what we were used to, but the voice had told me it was time. I was learning to trust myself. I knew that if the voice said it was time to move to California, it was time, and I went as fast as I could.

We moved to Orange County, and it forced me to level up as a businessman. As I said at the beginning of the book, you can't fake it in OC, or New York, or any other place where the prices are four to five times higher than elsewhere. You have to produce consistently and at high levels. You have to expand your mind-set and skill set.

Moving also forced me to level up as a father and a husband, because there is no family around here. It's just my wife, my boys, and me.

The voice guided me to do a few other things as I began working on this book: Launch the podcast (which hit number one on iTunes), write this book, conduct a live event for my clients, and lead a global revolution.

That voice inside you will speak to you according to your desires. It's easier to hear the voice prompting you when you are actively engaged in growth and progression toward your greatest purpose or holy cause. It's difficult to hear the voice when you are in park and have remained there for a long time. How do you activate that part of you? Make a choice and move.

Listening to the Silence

When the voice is absent and you are praying, fasting, or seeking guidance, and you hear nothing, view this as an answer, and that answer is for you to choose. You have the reins. You get to make a choice and then act on it.

I've seen many people lose out on opportunities because they waited for some divine inspiration to decide whom they should marry, where they should go to school, what type of job they should work, or what their higher purpose was. Choose. Make a choice and move, literally. Move your body; get into action. Just decide and then begin taking steps toward what you decide. No action means little or no guidance. As you take action on the decision that you've made, it becomes much easier to receive guidance from the voice—as opposed to waiting for the voice to come while you take no action. This has been the case every time in my life. I see it in my clients' lives too.

When I pray, fast, and meditate on an important decision and I receive no immediate guidance, I do my homework, look at every possibility, and then make a decision. You always have the ability to choose. Prosperity is a choice, and so is poverty. Happiness is a choice, and so is misery.

Choice is one of the greatest gifts we have as human beings. When we honor that gift of choice rather than asking Divine guidance to choose for us, we are more likely to receive the guidance we desire. Choose and move.

When I came home from the NFL, I was stunned. *What do I do now?* I prayed. I asked for help. And nothing came. I needed to make a decision and just move. I chose phone sales, and, after a time, I hated it and moved on. Then I discovered the mortgage industry, jumped in, and loved it for a season. I could have sat for months wondering, *What should I do?* or *Which job is right?* Instead, I made a choice and moved.

In dating or relationships, the only way to know if a person is the right fit for you—and you, for them—is to actually date the person. You make a choice and then figure it out as you go.

In business, many sit back and overanalyze what they should do for a marketing strategy, or whom they should hire. They go through all the pros and cons and spend weeks and months not making a decision, sitting in meetings and talking rather than doing. Inaction is very costly, and far more expensive than making an incorrect choice. In my experience, an incorrect choice is better than no choice because once you choose and get moving, you can make decisions and course-correct along the way. Figuring out if you're headed in the right direction is impossible from the boat harbor or from your garage. Launch the boat into the ocean. Put the car in gear and drive. Choose and move.

Listening and Responding

Some people call it the voice; some call it the spirit of God, the universe, or their gut. Whatever you call it, you must respond to it.

Can you learn to listen to that voice inside you?

Every time I've listened, I've prospered. Every time I haven't listened, I have failed. Nothing good comes when you ignore the voice. President of the LDS Church, Thomas S. Monson, says, "Never postpone a prompting." What has the voice been telling you to do in your life? What has it told you to do that you have you been avoiding? Can you listen to the voice?

Every time you listen, you're protected. Every time you listen, you prosper. Every time you don't listen, you lose. No matter how immediately gratifying it is not to listen, it's a no-win situation. And in the Prosperity Revolution, win-win is the only way to play.

I know that if you'll ask and listen, you'll receive. If you have courage to follow, you'll prosper. Following may mean it's time to write a book, start a business, move your family, go against the grain, or do something that may not make sense at the time.

Listening to the voice can mean walking away from a long-term relationship that has not served you and never will serve you. Listening may mean quitting activities that don't lead you to what you truly desire. Listening may sometimes mean going against the grain of what everyone else is doing.

What does the voice sound like or feel like? It feels peaceful. It often comes as thoughts, almost as if someone were speaking to you, and with those thoughts, the feeling inside confirms what you are hearing or picturing.

When the voice gives you a warning, it is distinct. You'll know it because it will pierce your heart and soul. It's not like the feeling that conveys, *Stay in bed because you are tired. Don't go work out.* The warning has always been so distinct that I know without a doubt it's that still, small voice telling me to stop, or to not go, or to avoid something. Whether or not we listen is up to us.

God is more eager to help us than we are to be helped by Him. If you don't believe in God, then believe in the universe or whatever that higher power or source is for you. I believe in God. I believe God. I know He is willing to help us and guide us to live our greatest purpose. No one benefits when you fail or play small. As an athlete, I don't want to win because someone shrank or contracted. When I play at my highest level, I want to beat the best.

When you shift the purpose of life from taking and consuming to expansion and value creation, you create new levels of possibility that never existed before.

Will you listen to the voice within?

What is it telling you to do? What is it telling you to stop doing? Whom is it telling you to follow? Whom is it telling you to stop following?

When it doesn't speak, make a choice and go. God can be involved in the intimate details of our lives if we choose it, listen, and follow.

Questions to Consider Carefully and Answer:

- Do you listen to the voice?
- When was the last time you felt or heard the voice?
- What did it tell you to do?
- What conditions allow the voice to be strong within you?
- How can you tell if it's you or the voice?

- Will you listen to the voice no matter how difficult or challenging it is?
- How does leveling up your environment give you greater opportunity to produce at higher levels?

CHAPTER 16

What's Next For You
In The Game Of Life?

|ıııı|ıııı|ıııı|ıııı|ıııı|ıııı|ıııı

*"The need of expansion is as genuine an instinct in
man as the need in a plant for the light. The love of
freedom is simply the instinct in man for expansion."*
—Matthew Arnold

It's always fun to read a book that changes your perspective, but inevitably we get to the end and ask ourselves, *"What's next?"*

So I ask, what's next for you? More specifically, what will you go out and **DO** as a result of the insights and distinctions you've experienced while reading this book?

What broken relationship will you heal?

What beautiful thing will you create?

What limiting behaviors will you choose to eliminate?

What powerful friendships will you cultivate?

What toxic influences will you cut off?

What thrilling dreams will you make a reality?

What unworkable stories will you get rid of and rewrite?

Most importantly, what must you do to become the most powerful version of YOU, the you that would create the impossible? What's your next step in living your greatest calling and winning again?

I ask because if you choose to stay content with the insights and distinctions you've learned in this book, you'll actually be worse off than if you'd never read the book. Getting clarity on what you must do in order to get what you want... and then making a choice to NOT DO IT is a serious and destructive act. It goes against universal principle and does not serve you or those you have the opportunity to influence.

So, I have some strong encouragement for you right now. Are you open to it? (By the way, it's worked for me without fail for the past 40 years and counting as well as working flawlessly for every single other person I've ever come in contact with - so I feel bold in sharing it with you.)

Here it is:

When you see clearly the thing that you must do — what I call your "next natural step" — Do it. Create it. Finish it. Make it happen. Make it real.

See the Thing & Do it and DO IT AFRAID.

You see, on my journey from scrapping for a spot on the high school football team to playing in the NFL, from making millions in mortgages and real estate to losing it all, from knocking doors in the summer heat to speaking on stages in front of thousands of people... there were so many moments where I desperately wanted to give up, to stop dreaming big, to settle and lie to myself that I was happy where I was, to pretend I didn't have a divine work to do.

This would have destroyed me and even in my darkest moments, I knew that there was a calling inside of me. The voice was always there whispering to me, *"Setema, the choice to settle is the choice to die."*

So, in every moment of darkness, when it seemed that every other light had gone out, I found that special unique light in my own heart and soul, a light that every human being has and... I made a choice.

Yes, it really was that simple. I CHOSE to get up and fight instead of giving up and settling. I CHOSE to continue to believe in myself. I CHOSE to act decisively in spite of my unwanted thoughts, feelings, emotions and moods. I saw my next step and I took it. I simply went out and did what was required and I'm still doing it every day. And when you're afraid, DO IT AFRAID. Just act. The fear rarely disappears. You simply act in spite of it, you do the next step afraid. Prosperity is a choice. And so is scarcity, mediocrity and poverty. I chose to prosper. What will you choose?

This is critical because if you really "want things to change" ... if you really want to live your greatest calling... if you really want to start winning again... then you're going to have to CHOOSE it and choose it again and again and again... every... single... day. It's called CHOOSE AND MOVE.

It truly is our simple daily choices that break through the inertia of the weak and purposeless lives we've been living for so long. The gravity of your small living will not let you go easily. You've got to stand up and CHOOSE to rise. That will be scary. The great news is that such a choice will, without fail, create entirely new possibilities and pathways for you to create the life you desire.

So, knowing this — are you going to choose your next step based on the limited and skewed view of what you thought was possible or impossible in the past? Of course not. Instead, you'll choose your next step based on the "Golden Thread" from the previous chapter — the work and the mission you feel the voice calling you to go out and do.

I know you'll have divine guidance and help every step of the way. The world moves for clear, committed people. The invisible hand helps those who get clear and committed. And even if you have a small tiny desire, choose it and the hand of providence will step in and assist. Not only will the right opportunities show up, they'll find their way to your day. The right people will show up in your life. The results that matter will come into reality, if you simply choose to do what's required for the desired result… if you CHOOSE to take the next step. Choose… and move.

So, what is it?

If you're mind says, "I'm not sure Setema," don't listen to it. Listen with your heart — your heart always knows what you really want, even if you're afraid to speak and declare it.

So, take time now before you close the cover, before our time here together ends and get clear on what you really want. What is your next step?

Write it down NOW and read it back to yourself every morning. If you're unwilling to do that, you're simply unwilling to do what's required to get what you want — which really means you don't really want it anyway. That's not you. Listen with your heart and your greatest desires will rise in a way that will inspire you. Do it now. Do it afraid. Do it regardless of circumstance or situation.

And now, as our time together in this book comes to an end, I have something else for you — a way for us to stay connected and keep the conversation of expansion going.

My Special Parting Gift to You

To help you stay clear and committed, I've created a very special gift for you. It's my sincerest gift to you for buying this book and reading it through to the end.

It includes a collection of my most powerful and impactful audio presentations — recordings of special live trainings where I shared the principles of the Prosperity Revolution in full and in order.

This special audio training library will help you see in yourself new levels of power and leadership. It also contains a power pack of templates, scripts, cheat sheets and checklists to kick-start your journey unlike anything you've experienced before.

The retail value of this training is over well over $497 and you can go get it all right now by simply visiting this link:

www.WinningAftertheGame.com/mygift

You only get one life on this earth and if you do it right, that's more than enough. You have the opportunity to impact, inspire and lead others with every breath you take. So, do it now. You can win again, in every part of life, every single day. The world is waiting for YOU. Not the small you. Not the "aw shucks" you. Not the "who am I to think I could do that" you.

No, the world is waiting for the real you, the powerful you. The powerful, clear, committed, loving YOU. Choose to be that version of yourself every day for the next 90 days and I can promise you, your world will be completely unrecognizable from the one you live in today.

The Prosperity Revolution has begun and you get to choose to be a part of it.

To your success and your happiness.

To you winning again in your life.

To your holy cause.

Love you,

Setema Gali

The Reverend of the Revolution

Morgan James
Speakers Group

🔊 www.TheMorganJamesSpeakersGroup.com

We connect Morgan James published
authors with live and online events
and audiences whom will benefit
from their expertise.